Kicking Leaves

To Don + Nadine,
    To love and laughs —
        Capentos Tissot
        6-29-18

Also by Caperton Tissot

The Beat Within;
Poetry, Another Round, 2017

Adirondack Flashes and Floaters;
A River of Verse, 2014

Saranac Lake's Ice Palace;
a History of Winter Carnival's Crown Jewel, 2012

Tibetta's World;
High Jinks and Hard Times in the North Country, 2012

Adirondack Ice;
a Cultural and Natural History, 2010

History Between the Lines;
Women's Lives and Saranac Lake Customs, 2007

More Information and contact at www.SnowyOwlPress.com

Kicking Leaves

THE CONTRARIAN LIFE
OF A YANKEE REBEL

A Memoir

Caperton Tissot

ISBN: 978-1-387-82160-0

PublishNation LLC
www.publishnation.net

For those who follow

In this fast-paced world
Oral traditions fade
Online words quickly come and go
But stories in print are stories saved –
For those who follow
Caperton Tissot

Thanks

A big thanks to my beloved husband who, once more with meticulous care, edited and fine tuned my words. I am also greatly indebted to that special Tuesday night gang of writers who inspired me to undertake this book. Thanks to Steven Sonnenberg, MD, who took the photo in the "Welcome" section. And last but not least, there would be no story without my family and friends. I have been lucky to have so many good people in my life, shoring me up when I am down, laughing with me when things go well, and encouraging me to keep on writing. I have not been alone on my journey.

Text Note:

Many friends know my husband as Will. He Americanized his name to Will after a number of years in this country because, he said, few could pronounce Wim correctly. However, he will always be Wim to me. And so, in this account, that is how I refer to him.

Welcome

Prime me with a nod and stories spill out like water from a pump; they're mostly short, but not this time. Here is the story of my life.

Born in Worcester, MA, I grew up in the 1940s and '50s with the proverbial silver spoon wedged firmly in my mouth. An independent child, I slowly slid away from my roots, eventually finding delight in the defiant and hope-filled '60s. From that time on, I bounced from one place to another, both figuratively and literally – to and from various locations as well as cultures. I write this memoir in the hope that it will give future generations insight into, not only my life, but its historical context.

A second reason to write: telling stories brings order to chaos. While storytellers entertain (a stage trick to hide the inner self), here, I not only share the good times but lift the curtain to afford readers a peek backstage.

Life, however, is not always on stage; it is far from the stage as well. At those times, I've wandered from the trodden path, curiosity leading me astray. Bushwhacking was not easy, but regrets are few. Of hard days there were plenty, but good ones as well.

I believe in having fun whenever possible. I laugh a lot. But an optimist I am not – rather an *opportunist* who tries to make the best of whatever comes my way. Hopefully, you will relate to the ups and downs – for we all suffer, all laugh and, in retrospect, all too often take ourselves more seriously than we should.

CHAPTER 1

Rough Road: Home to Boarding School

"What do you mean I can't have a martini?" Those naive words came directly out of the mouth of a 15-year-old girl not used to being contradicted, and certainly not by a waiter. The year was 1956 and I was sitting with my parents in a Providence, Rhode Island, restaurant, eating my "last supper" before getting on the night train to make the long trip back to incarceration in a boarding school in rural Virginia. I had always needed a drink to ease climbing the steps into that Pullman car. My parents, unaware I wanted this extra boost to help face the coming months, had never objected. Cocktail hour was a normal evening ritual at home, though one I did not always participate in. Maybe this was the beginning of checking young people's age before serving alcohol, or maybe I had, happenchance, not been challenged before. After all, my family never took me to anything so "vulgar" as a public restaurant, unless forced to by the necessity of travel. For us, eating out meant going to the old brick Worcester Club building where lush wisteria climbed the outside walls and a ring of the doorbell brought a butler who greeted us each by name; or else it meant driving to the Tatnuck Country Club, that was situated far away from residential or business areas so that, in its idyllic location, the riff-raff were not likely to happen by.

In my well-protected life, I was indignant to be denied a martini. Nevertheless, to my astonishment, not even my parents could talk their way around the age obstacle; I had to submit to civic law and go dry. After dinner, however, I, the duty-bound child, did what was expected and got on the train without fuss. Settling into a private sleeping room, I pulled down my bed, tucked in for the overnight ride, and imagined my parents' late-hour quiet drive home, anticipating a resumption of their child-free life together. As the train rumbled through the night, I dreamed about staying on board right past my station and riding the rails straight through to that glorious mysterious place called "The West." I was completely alone and realized it was possible, nothing was stopping me. I could disappear somewhere and how could they ever find me? But I was still too obedient a child and lacked the will.

I yearned to find the real world and the people that lived in it. How did they earn their living? Why did they make wrong decisions resulting in poverty when by just doing the right thing, they, too, could have the easy life so many of us enjoyed? ... Or so I was told. These puzzling questions had ridden on my shoulders since, as an 8-year-old, I had read *The Prince and the Pauper* by Mark Twain. In that story, a prince and pauper exchange roles. I was introduced to the idea that good fortune comes more from the luck of birth than our own noble virtue. As a result, I had told Mother (or Mummy as I used to call her) that I wanted to be poor when I grew up, thinking maybe then I could better understand how those poverty-stricken folks endured, and why they "chose" to live as they did. Mother, proud of her heritage, cringed at hearing her only daughter's curious ambition.

Arriving in Washington, D.C., the next morning, gutlessly submissive, I disembarked from the train as expected. I did treat myself, however, by doing what I always did on these trips through the Capital: I escaped for a few solitary hours to explore my favorite place, the Smithsonian Institution. It was heavenly and no matter how many times I went, it was never enough. Filled with history, science and nature, it appealed to all that fascinated me. I had grown up in mostly lonely circumstances (my brothers, 3 and 5 years older, were soon off to prep school), had spent much of my youth either reading or tramping through the woods, jackknife in my pocket, ready to dissect stems, leaves and flowers to discover their inner essence. Early on, I had resisted being Mother's little princess – a cutely dressed toddler smiling and pleasing adults. I had become a scruffy child with long braids, happiest in blue jeans; always anxious to get away into the forest.

At the age of 11, I created a natural history museum, published a nature newsletter and devoted myself to studying wildlife. I was, therefore, fascinated by the spectacular world inside the Smithsonian. Engrossed in discoveries, I found the hours melted away all too quickly. Suddenly, it would be late afternoon and time to return for the final train ride to my school.

There was always a great kabumpus at the train platform as girls flew into each other's arms, screaming with excitement after their "long" separation. It was as if we had been absent from each other for years instead of just a couple of weeks, or at the most the two and a half months of summer break. I was slightly put off by the excessive enthusiasm, especially as returning to school was not my idea of fun.

Finally, late in the day, the train arrived at the village where the school was located. This institution of learning was exactly what one might imagine an exclusive, southern female preparatory school to look like: an ivy covered red brick chapel, gymnasium, library, and two three-story buildings connected by an enclosed arcade whose walls were laced with windows that opened wide on warm days to let the breeze blow through.

2

The main building was fronted by tall white columns supporting a high roofed porch. French doors led into a large elegant front hall in the main building. Upholstered furniture in muted blues and grays, a soft carpet and gold framed original paintings made up the genteel setting. A wide staircase rose to the second and third floors where balconies circled the downstairs hall. From these observation decks, girls could gaze down on the activity below, making sure they missed nothing of social importance. Sometimes, I would stand there by myself, late at night, and peer down over the white railings edging these circular halls. I had the sensation of being on the lip of a vortex that was sucking me around and around, down deeper and deeper. I was mesmerized and eased back toward the wall, unnerved at feelings I could not grasp.

Academically, the school was one of the best in the country. Classes were small, strictly run. Homework was extensive, requiring that we study most afternoons when not in gym, and at least two more hours in the evening. Any assignments that couldn't be finished were worked on over the weekend. I don't remember extra help or tutoring being offered. I think you survived or flunked. Rarely did that happen though, because the selection process for acceptance was pretty stringent. One needed, for the most part, to come from a fair amount of wealth, be bright, and in possession of the right family background. The student body, about 130 girls, hailed mostly from urban areas in the Northeast, a few from the West and Midwest, an occasional Southerner, and in the mix, to show what a cosmopolitan institution it purported to be, a rare overseas or South American, carefully screened, fairly white-skinned exchange student. Three or four town girls were slipped into our midst, but they were "mere locals" not deserving serious attention from classmates. I wonder how they endured it all.

So what were our days like? Here is what I remember. We woke each morning to the first of many jarringly loud bells reverberating through all the buildings the rest of the day until the final "lights out bell" announced our freedom to sleep and escape into dreams; a robotic, bell-controlled swarm of young women under the illusion that we were maturing into free thinking, well-educated members of the universe, or at least of the only society that counted.

We lived two, occasionally three, to a room. Those rooms were about 15 feet long and 10 feet wide, with a bed, chest of drawers, desk, lamp and chair for each girl. Daily inspection ensured that our beds were made with matching bedspreads, no wrinkles, no more than one pillow and one stuffed animal perched on top, a total of five objects on the chest of drawers, one bulletin board to which we could attach no more than ten items at a time, one acceptable pair of curtains in the windows, two books

3

on the desk, pencils, and other paraphernalia organized neatly in a desk drawer, closet and drawers in order with no more than the allowed amount of clothing stored neatly within. Radios and phonographs were strictly forbidden. Hiding such in your room was cause for expulsion. Computers had not yet come into existence. Living in military barracks would have been a picnic after that kind of training. At the clang of the first morning bell, we got up, showered in the shared bathrooms that had five shower stalls, several sinks and a row of toilet cubicles with curtains in front of each. Not being used to the South, I was startled one day to sit on the toilet, whip the curtain across the front and be faced with my first cockroach, well over 3 inches long. I had always studied and loved the northern butterfly and bug world, but this added a new dimension to my knowledge of entomology. After this experience, in spite of my love of nature, I was careful to check the curtain before entering a stall.

We had a half-hour to get dressed and downstairs to breakfast. That was all we needed as makeup and jewelry were forbidden. Without such accoutrements, it took little time to prepare. For us, it was shirts and skirts, bobby-sox and saddle shoes.

We all ate together in a large dining room filled with white linen-draped tables, each seating usually seven students and one faculty member. Seats were assigned; we sat in the same place for breakfast, lunch, and dinner, then after a month, moved to a new table with different students. Announcements and a blessing preceded each meal.

In addition to cleaning our rooms, Blacks in uniforms waited on tables. We were discouraged from talking with those who served, except to say thank you or ask for more food, and so those silent figures, so much a part of our daily life, acquired a degree of mystery. Rumor was that parents of some had been slaves. We suspected that several lived in houses on the vast school/ farm property, but as most of that land was off-limits, we never knew for sure. In any case, they were there to serve, not to socialize, so, to my regret, we didn't give them a whole lot of thought.

However, there was one rather good-looking young waiter who we used to imagine, and hope, was often staring at us. A dessert called floating islands was occasionally served, consisting of yellow pudding with puffs of whipped egg whites topped with red cherries. We were sure we saw this man roll his eyes and smirk at the resemblance to our breasts…or did we dream this up? After all, and except for two older male teachers and the headmaster, we had no contact with the opposite sex for months at a time.

When it came to dining, I have never again been treated to such feasting. Three times a day, seven days a week, we "ladies" were indulged with food for the gods. It went a long way toward compensating for other things that I began to realize, were seriously missing in our lives.

After breakfast, we prepared our rooms for inspection then docilely marched through our predestined day, driven by the harsh buzz of bells marking the schedule of morning classes, lunch, more classes, afternoon gym, evening chapel, dinner, study hall and bed.

At this Episcopal school, evening chapel was mandatory. The headmaster, also a minister, delivered lectures, reminding us that we were not to lower ourselves by speaking to the boys in town from the military academy, nor, for that matter, to give too much attention to any of the army of black servants who did our laundry, cleaned our rooms, cooked our food, worked on the school farm, maintained the gardens, and in every way labored to spare our virginal lives from exposure to the realities of the outside world. It was 1957 and segregation was in full swing: separate everything from drinking fountains to lunch counters. It was "back of the bus" ridership for thousands. Prejudice was preached from the pulpit. Just to make sure we didn't slip and fall into disgrace, several tactics were employed.

In the first place, we attended a full day of school on Saturdays. This prevented us from strolling into the village at a time when farmers and other locals might be encountered. However, we were allowed, if we had good grades and no demerits, to walk into the village on Mondays when most residents had gone back to work. That required we sign up in advance, leave at a specific time, sign in with the chaperone in the village, enter only certain stores, and return to school within two hours, signing back in, of course. Fear of earning demerits by breaking the rules and speaking to the "wrong" folks prevented me from saying so much as "excuse me" should I bump into a passerby on the sidewalk.

The pleasures I derived from this privilege were: one, walking down the hill away from our ivory towered estate, enjoying the sight of the woods, trees and fields along the way; and two, eating sumptuous malt sundaes at the drugstore soda fountain. What ever happened to malt? It was a flavor made in heaven. In fact, whatever happened to soda fountains?

With vacation approaching, the school staff would be in a tizzy at the prospect of our sharing transportation with such characters as soldiers, salesmen, or other "questionable" inhabitants of the planet. Fortunately for them, these trips home happened rarely. We were sprung from confinement only for Christmas, spring break and summer. Elaborate plans were laid out to prevent mishaps from taking place on the bus, train and plane trips. Chaperones were flung in every direction. It didn't matter if you were traveling as far as 1,000 miles east, west, north, or south, eyes

5

were upon you. They needn't have worried so much as it was recommended that we openly carry the *Atlantic Monthly*, on the assumption that anyone seeing that accessory would not dare approach.

So off we set, after singing a song in the dining room each evening for the preceding two weeks. To the tune of *The Bear Went over the Mountain,* we belted out "Fourteen days to vacation, off we go to the station" counting down each night to lift off. On the final day, everyone arose, ready to leave by 6 AM. We faced trips of anywhere from eight hours to two days.

What excitement as the New York train streamed north. I watched out the window for the first sight of snow piles, signs we were approaching the temperamental seasons of Massachusetts countryside in whose woods and meadows I had grown up. The landscape around our school was beautiful as well, great spreading trees, brilliant flowers and lovely clipped hedges. But, like the school it encompassed, nothing wild or spontaneous had a place in this cultivated environment. I struggled to find out where I fit into the scheme of things.

At home for Christmas, I attended a couple of dances. I was not invited by a date but driven there by my parents or occasionally another girl's parents. I was no wallflower, as the saying goes, I was the whole vine. My mother had made me a hope chest into which I was supposed to start collecting linens and silverware for the day I would get married. My older brother, Robin (Rodney Jr.), called it my "hopeless chest." He was not far off the mark. Social life did not go smoothly. Then a wise friend, only 15 years old, opened my eyes. "People don't want to hear from you, they want to tell you about themselves. If you become a good listener, you'll have no problem getting along." Her words have lived with me to this day.

I first left for boarding school at age 15, entering into my sophomore year. I'd come from a private day school in the city. We lived in a large house in Worcester, MA, within easy walking distance of a private school named Bancroft, the only school I had ever attended. Three events stand out from those early years: first, in second grade I tried to cheat on a spelling test by writing F-I-R-E in very light letters on a piece of paper so I could refer to it when needed. I got caught – my first and last time – at cheating, that is. Then, I remember in the third grade, reading a book about the sea that was taken away from me because the teacher said it was too difficult. And last, in 1954 when the words "under God" were added to the Pledge of Allegiance, I refused to say them. "Wasn't all mankind under God?" I asked. "Why did we think America had a monopoly on blessings?"

I enjoyed playing in our city backyard, but what I really looked forward to was spending weekends and vacations at our rather primitive country camp some 25 miles away. The camp, or I should say camps, for we had two, one used in the summer and one in the winter, were on Brooks Pond near North Brookfield, MA. Our camps were surrounded by acres of woods, fields, and a few other scattered second homes. I could never understand why we had to live between three different houses. If one is better than the others, why not just live there and save all the wasted travel time? When I grew up, I planned to live in one place and one place only. The country setting was the one I loved best and that I extensively explored, studying the natural world around me.

By the age of 12, I was practicing the art of taxidermy, using an array of road kill picked up by friends and delivered to our freezer. I displayed these in my museum, along with a rather extensive butterfly collection. I also exhibited pressed flowers and ferns, freshwater shells, a variety of donated fossils, snake skins, turtle shells, skulls and homemade dioramas showing the various stages of forest development.

Less impressive was another of my ventures. I had wanted to raise honeybees and finally obtained a wooden hive box and bees. On suiting up to go open the hive for maintenance, I put on boots, long pants, long sleeves, gloves and a head-net. My friend Becky went along to help. We had no protection for her so she made do with a straw hat, a dishtowel hung over it, no gloves and sandals. Becky was calm and relaxed. I was not. Bees sense those things. They sniffed a scaredy-cat and immediately attacked with glee – me, not Becky. They managed to get inside my boots, pants, shirt and netting, drilling into my skin without mercy and sending me fleeing. It brought my beekeeping to a stinging end.

At age 14, I took up a new activity – figure skating – encouraged by my parents, who were members of a figure skating club. We had grown up skating on Brooks Pond, often going out in our bathrobes early in the morning to visit with the ice fishermen. It was great fun – the sound of our skates cutting the ice, the surrounding snow covered hills, the crisp dawn air. Sometimes I used to drag a sled full of fishing equipment and skate off for a day of ice fishing by myself. I'd build a fire to keep warm and wait for the red flags on my tip-ups to spring to life when a fish bit. I never caught much, but loved the adventure. Skating on hard natural ice, however, is different from skating on the softer surface in an arena. Indoors, I developed a desire to advance my skills. I was privileged to skate with Dick Button (Olympic medal winner) and Frank Carroll (Olympic coach of medal winners). I passed several required tests for competition, both in figure and ice dancing, and participated in several local ice shows. My mother sewed a lovely velvet green short-skirted costume for exhibitions. I developed a solo routine to the music of a Strauss waltz. This was a serious avocation. At 6 AM, at least three mornings a week, my dedicated parents would drive me to the ice rink across town where I practiced for two hours before being driven to school.

When I entered my freshman year of Bancroft, I was acutely disappointed at the teaching. It seemed simplistic and empty. In addition, my brother Henry was living at home struggling with his own problems. He'd been sent off to boarding school several times in an effort to straighten him out, but with a strong personality and a rebellious streak (similar to mine but far more courageous), he rejected their efforts to point him in the "right" direction. He was expelled from Tabor Academy and St. George's, much to his delight. Home life was not so smooth. He and I fought constantly, so I decided it best to go away. I should have been paying closer attention to his reaction to boarding schools, but at that point, I was more influenced by my parents and my brother Robin who had always been kind to me. He successfully attended boarding school and later Williams College, seeming to enjoy it all. I guess I was trying to follow in his footsteps.

My mother, a Virginian, had raised us on stories of her aristocratic background, her preference for the "more refined" Southerners over vulgar small-town Northerners. "You need to get out of the North and find out what southern living is like," she told me. Ever obedient to my parents, I thought she was probably right. I did occasionally visit my cousin Lisa in Staunton, VA, and I always had a good time. To be fair, my parents first took me to visit a small country boarding school in New Hampshire. I remember falling in love with it. I would have enrolled there at once, but was strongly advised not to because it was "not academically good enough." I was persuaded instead to choose the "better" southern school. Big mistake.

I never visited the institution but was assured I would love it. And so, leaving behind my independent life of reading, skating and nature studies, I set off to discover how people lived in other parts of the world, that other part being *The South.*

The first year, I was rather awed by the elegance of my surroundings, the privilege of being in one of America's top preparatory schools and the "sophisticated" girls who filled my new world. In addition to the school buildings, the campus included flower gardens, small faculty houses, an indoor pool, riding stables, riding rings, fields and somewhere out of bounds, housing for the staff and a large farm. A long driveway lined with massive ancient trees circled in front of the main buildings.

The school was a community unto itself. I think it was the first time I had ever been a part of a social group.

At home, due to constantly moving back and forth from the country to the city during fall, winter and spring, my parents socialized little and I had seen few other kids. But, in the summer, there had been weekly cocktail parties with seven or eight families that had their second homes around the upper or "acceptable" end of the lake. Those parties took place on Sundays following sailing canoe races. Right after the races, my dad used miniature aluminum sailing boats to point out each of my mistakes and how they could have been avoided. His intentions were good, but nevertheless the sessions ended with me in tears.

After those lessons, I was expected to pull myself together, put a smile on my face and, with the family, paddle across the lake to whichever camp was hosting the after-race party. As a very young child, I had enjoyed the parties. We kids used to play games swim and hang out together. As I grew older, I dreaded these affairs. I just didn't fit in anymore. My parents were politically ultra conservative. On the strength of a few drinks, they seemed to enjoy antagonizing all their friends. Afterward, we would paddle back home in stony silence.

More fun were the schooner trips enjoyed a few times off Cape Cod. I loved watching the patterns of sea waves, hearing the wind whistle in the sails, listening to the bow slicing through the ocean and smelling the salty air. It was on one of these trips that I, at the age of 12, was deemed old enough to take over the wheel while my brothers, my dad and the captain went below for naps. As we sailed along, I happened to notice a stick coming out of the water 30 feet from the boat. Uh-oh, was it that shallow here?

The stick, however, seemed to be moving at the speed of our boat. Suddenly a full-sized submarine exploded out of the ocean, water cascading off its hull. I shrieked, sure the Communists had come to get us as my John Bircher father had always told me they would.

Then a hatch on the conning tower burst open and a uniformed officer popped up with a megaphone hollering "Get that boat the hell out of here immediately!" The captain and my family came pouring up on deck to see what was happening. The problem was soon apparent. We had sailed into restricted naval territory. Later, they had a good hard laugh about it. I failed to find it humorous at all. Fun as the trips were, I took no friends along. It was just Dad, the captain and my brothers, who had each other for company. I was usually the odd (girl) out.

Sailing was a big part of my father and Henry's life. My father designed a 24-foot-long deep draft sharpie and together, over a period of three years, they brought the design to life by building a seaworthy, single-masted ocean vessel named the *Chewink*. Henry sailed it for several years off Cape Cod. Occasionally I took trips with him. Taking his friends along, we traveled from one harbor to another – playing ukuleles, singing, going for swims and generally enjoying a carefree time. I loved the adventure.

But other than that, as a teen, my social life was limited. Our country homes, comfortable but modest houses, were 4 miles from North Brookfield. I understood the village was a place where you were to be polite, but not interact too closely with the locals. We would never have thought of befriending them. There, we purchased groceries and building supplies, but never clothes.

When still quite young, I had two loyal girlfriends. They were endlessly criticized by my parents. This led me to find fault with them as well – on no grounds whatsoever. My very best friend was Becky. Her family lived close to us in the city and summered on Brooks Pond as did we. Our friendship went back as far as I can remember. We built forts, explored the woods, paddled and swam, had picnics and sometimes camped out. In the city we played in our backyards and on a dead end street. We roller-skated and rolled hoops; an activity considered obsolete even back then. I treated her poorly; criticizing her at every turn and making her kill all the spiders in our clubhouse. She recalls that, at my instigation, we once made a playmate lick the street. I was jealous of Becky. She was cute, friendly and likeable – all the things I was not. I wonder why she ever stuck with me.

That encompassed all the community I had known before going away to school. At first, being part of the southern culture was thrilling. I studied hard, tried to behave and for the first year, didn't let on that the dean of the school was my aunt: my mother's sister.

One of the skills that well-bred girls were expected to acquire was that of horseback riding and not western saddle either, that was "too common." English saddle – that flat plate of leather on which you try to balance five feet up in the air while a willful animal careens about underneath. Until this time, my experience with riding had not been promising. In Massachusetts, my parents used to drop me off, along with one of my friends, for two of three hours at a horse trading stable, then come back and retrieve the pieces. I don't think, at least I hope, they were not in the least aware of what took place in their absence. This was clearly before liability concern raised its ugly head.

The stable was not so much a riding center as a horse trading barn. The owner simply made a few bucks on the side with a rent-a-horse operation. Neither my friend nor I had the least idea how to sit on a horse, but in our hopeful exuberance, we continued to try. The owner made us pay up front in case we did not survive our ventures. He then grabbed a couple of horses, whichever happened to be available for trade on that particular day, saddled them up, pointed us in the direction of some trails and told us what time to be back.

The horses came in a variety of shapes, heights and temperaments. Some were circus retirees, some had seen better days on the race track, and some were just darn right mean, with good reason I'm sure. We would lead them to a rock or fence, struggle to get on board and take off. I remember these long-legged beasts suddenly dropping to their knees and rolling over in an effort to erase us annoying 12-year-olds off their backs, as if we were nothing more than bothersome flies. Once, our horses raced each other down a road, two abreast and completely out of control. When a car came around the corner, the horses careened off to the side and we riders careened straight down onto the tarmac, forcing the driver to slam on his brakes to avoid running us over. Other times, our fierce beasts of burden would dash through the woods, attempting to wipe us off on passing trees, or decapitate us by sliding beneath overhanging branches. One time, as my horse suddenly plunged down a steep hill, I was catapulted into a tall tree growing up from below. Embarrassed, I had to scramble 10 feet down to reach the ground. We did eventually learn to stay glued as needed and to bail out when in danger. None of it was particularly relaxing. Those were adrenalin-pumping events. Then, one day I suddenly decided the odds of survival were getting ever worse, that horses just couldn't be trusted, and I vowed never more to climb on board again. That was my thinking when I arrived at the boarding school. "I'm not ever riding again," I announced. "I don't trust horses."

"Nonsense," I was told, you just need to learn to ride *correctly*, how to take control." That made some sense, but I was still reluctant.

"I just don't trust horses," I repeated. Disregarding my protest, the school staff informed me that if I rode correctly, everything would be delightful. The following week found me properly attired in jodhpurs, tall black riding boots and a white blouse that was totally inappropriate for riding about in the red dusty Virginian countryside. However, with laundry service provided, southern ladies didn't need to bother their heads with such thoughts. We beginners walked our horses sedately around the fence as we watched an expert student equestrian in the middle of the ring demonstrate how to ride. In midair, at the height of her gallop, the horse suffered a heart attack and dropped like a bullet, slamming into the dirt and throwing his rider the length of the ring and through the rails. She rolled down the field like tumbleweed, breaking her arm and collarbone. Her horse twitched so badly, the stable manager was summoned to shoot it. All the while, the rest of us continued to ride primly around the perimeter trying to pretend there was no dead animal lying in our midst, or that our classmate was being hauled away for repairs. This was my last ride. It served to reinforce my belief, beyond a doubt, that you can just never trust a horse.

If we didn't participate in riding, the usual team sports were available. I don't remember that any water was provided as we warmed up running around the sports field under the blazing southern sun. That was before wearing hats and sufficient hydration was deemed important. Frequently suffering terrible stomach cramps, dizziness and faintness, I was allowed to leave the field and return to my room, always surprised at how easily I got dismissed. The coach must have understood what was happening, but I didn't. I would suffer terrible diarrhea and headaches. Sometimes, I thought I wouldn't be able to make it back to my dorm, but no one came with me to help. Physical ailments were taken seriously, but brought no pampering.

My dad passed along the notion that those who teach do so because they are unfit for any other profession. This warped attitude was hardly helpful. I had a deep sense of curiosity and love of learning, but his influence made me argumentative in the classroom, too often with a closed mind to the lessons of the day. It was only in later years, when married to a teacher, that I developed a healthy respect for educators.

Despite a tendency toward quarrelsomeness, I was an honor roll student. This feat earned little or no praise from my family for the same reason they did not react when I was elected to the position of student council member. Most would consider these two accomplishments of some note. Other parents congratulated their children; mine did not. I finally phoned home, thinking they had not heard the news. Yes, they had been informed, but they expected nothing less so what was the need for congratulations?

I came from a family with a curious mix of beliefs. While Mother tried to raise me to be socially acceptable, Dad rather focused on teaching me to be independent, think for myself and take responsibility for my actions. His mother died when he was a boy; his father, rather aloof, died when he was newly married. He had grown up essentially on his own, necessarily having to think for himself. He wanted to teach us to do the same. Our winter weekends were spent at our country place, called The Barn (its original purpose). Because Mother often preferred staying in the city, we were under Dad's supervision which was no supervision at all. It's "liberty hall," he said. You can do what you want, go where you wish, eat when you're hungry – the only rules: you must clean up whatever mess you make, including dirty dishes; not do anything dangerous, or if you do, at least be smart enough to get yourself out of the fix.

Typical of his approach to parenting was an event that took place at our city house when I was 11 years old. My parents had gone out for the evening. I went to bed, only to be awoken by the smell of smoke. I checked the whole house, even the dark basement, which was extremely scary. Finding no fire, I phoned my parents to ask what to do. Dad answered. "If you're worried the house is on fire, go sleep by the door." And so I did. Dragging my hamster, bird and dog with me, I curled up on the floor in the front hall where he and Mother later found me. She was furious at my dad for not telling her I had called.

I was raised not to be afraid, but sometimes fear got the better of me. Then I turned to reading as a distraction. When I was young and my parents went out for the evening, I was faced with a dilemma. I was scared: scared when my brothers got mad at me and scared when they weren't there and I was left alone. My solution was to lock myself in the bathroom where I resorted to reading a stash of books kept hidden in the top of a tall cupboard. Stories would fill the evening until I heard my parents pull into the driveway. Then, knowing it was safe to come out, I would hop into bed and pretend to be asleep

Dad instilled in us the belief that you only ask for help if it is absolutely not possible to solve the problem yourself. I rarely asked for anything. Television had not yet invaded many homes, ours included, to assault children with advertising. I did not know about all the things I was supposed to want. On the rare occasions when I did ask for a particular toy, he would answer, "Why don't you make it?" He helped me with projects that included everything from boats, to dollhouse furniture, and even one time, a doll. We made her from a piece of pine, a 2-by-4, its stick legs and arms attached with screw eyes. Mother, in despair over this unwieldy creature, later helped me make a soft one, actually a marionette. I stuffed and converted a sock, insisting it be black, into a Negro boy. I don't remember her objecting to the color. We sewed on the face, hair, and clothes, then attached it to strings from a T-shaped wooden handle. In fact, Mother bought me the first doll I ever remember having. That too, I insisted be black. Once more, muting her prejudice, she did not object, though she must have wondered why I wanted black dolls. I chose them simply because I found them prettier than white ones.

For the most part, things my mother found important differed from those of my father. My parents, in marrying each other, made a valiant attempt to reconcile their northern and southern roots. Only in later years did I come to understand that I, like them, was also influenced by family history, though mine took the form of rebellion rather than compliance.

Mother diligently shouldered the responsibility of ensuring that everyone knew our aristocratic Virginian background. In carrying out her crusade, she not only isolated herself, rejecting opportunities to make good friends, but passed a heavy burden of social elitism on to me. On the one hand, I was highly critical of everyone who walked or talked. On the other hand, coming from such a "distinguished" family, it was impossible to have an identity of my own.

Mother suffered this same conflict, though never consciously. For her, men were superior to women. She defined her position in society based on the important males in her lineage. She trusted no professional who was a woman. The tragedy of this thinking, learned presumably at her mother's knee, was that it left her with little means of defining her own identity. Though highly intelligent with a good mind, she rarely put it to use outside the house. But, she never complained either. In her social station, one presented only a confident and carefully controlled exterior. Mother was a product of her culture, as was my aunt. One day, in my junior year, feeling terribly unhappy, I broke down and for the first time went to consult my aunt (the dean), pouring out my problems and confessing to desperate depression. She listened in silence, then after a pause said, "The hem of your skirt is crooked. You need to fix that." Appearance was everything. Conversation over, I was dismissed.

We all travel with baggage; this was the nature of mine. I dragged my heritage along to boarding school where I was expected to carry it with pride. It didn't happen. Perhaps I'd already spent too much solitude as a child, reading and reflecting on the nature of things. After one year of indoctrination into the finer points of southern living, recollections of *The Prince and the Pauper* started to re-emerge. By what merit had any of us risen to the exalted status we were told we deserved? How could this be a Christian approach to the world? Wasn't there something in there about "Blessed are the poor?" Was grinding poverty really so blessed? The oppressed were no more deserving of their fate than the wealthy of theirs. I shared my thinking with no one, unable to find classmates with similar concerns. Disillusionment grew.

My lineage weighed upon me. It was suffocating, reaching down through generations to demand I live by its values. How could I become anything more than a conduit for a long line of ancestors who included a judge, doctor, statesman, signer of the Declaration of Independence, bank presidents and family members who had Tiffany windows dedicated to them? When my mother married and set off for the North, her own father's last words of advice were: "Never give up the servants." With such a past, I felt my own frail identity slipping away. I began the lonely struggle to carve out a new path.

In boarding school, we were expected to learn the importance of community service by signing up for one of several pre-selected activities. I chose to work at a daycare center for Blacks. My school picked the center, the time to go there, how often we went, what we would do on arrival and how long we stayed, then bused us back to our dorms. Submitting to this done deal indicated our great sense of responsibility. Those running the daycare, we were informed, were deeply grateful for our help. I wondered. Something about the scheme was off key. Who were those children? Why the shabby building? Where were the all the toys? Segregation was in full swing. How did the teachers feel about this bunch of privileged white teenagers descending on their premises, showing them how things should be done? I dared not ask the questions. I sank deeper into solitude.

Finally, the culmination of my unhappiness flowed over. Why must I attend an elite college? Why couldn't we speak to the Blacks? Why were we reassured every day, in fact from the very pulpit of our Episcopal chapel, that we were superior to everyone else? How much longer could I bear being herded about with such unquestioning submission? Why must there be a dress code, no other clothes accepted? We received an excellent education because our parents could afford it. What about those who couldn't?

My S.A.T. scores, expected to rise from junior to senior year, dropped dramatically. However, I was still on the honor roll and thus allowed to work in my room during the two-hour evening study hall. One of the school rules allowed us to hang a sign on our bedroom door that said "white flag." Nobody was to knock and disturb you except for your roommate. I always hung the sign in the evening. It afforded me the privacy I so craved and helped me bear up. Not that I didn't have friends, I did. But the lack of solitude depressed me as well as living a life regulated by bells and stifling societal rules. Little was left to our own choice. Each morning after breakfast we were even instructed whether or not to wear a sweater or jacket that day. Breaking the recommendation, even just to dash across the arcade from one building to another, meant demerits and possible loss of the privilege of studying in one's own room or walking to town once a month. I couldn't wait to graduate and leave.

The highlight of every day was the chance at 10 A.M. to rush to the windowed door in front of our post office boxes. I would peer through, praying, "Please, please, please, let there be a letter for me!" The fronts of the post boxes were glass and we would look for the diagonal line cutting corner to corner indicating that mail had come. We had to wait until after lunch to collect it. Mother, despite disappointment with her daughter, loved me very much and wrote often with all the news from home. Hearing from her was my salvation. That was almost my only communication with the outside world. Her letters were comforting, very much as she had been in my youth during the many nights she sat with me as I gasped for another asthmatic breath.

Only telephone calls from parents were allowed. An operator ran the switchboard, located in the back of the great hall. If your parents wanted to call, it had to be arranged beforehand so you could be waiting near the three phone booths next to her desk. That didn't happen often. There were no TV's, no radios, nor did we go to movies. For news, we subscribed to either *Newsweek* or *Time*, I don't remember which. But with such an ivory tower lifestyle, it was hard to come down off the pedestal and relate to events taking place outside our small domain.

Instruction was excellent. The subjects were not unusual, but the intensity and depth of study was. I don't know statistics but believe that every one of us continued on to rather prestigious colleges, many already accepted in their junior year. I was expected to attend Smith College, my aunt's alma mater, but by that time, lights had started to come on in the darkroom of my brain.

CHAPTER 2

Breaking Free

During the summer after my junior year, I moved to Boston, taking a job as a teller replacing vacationing employees at various banks. Such respectable work suited me poorly. I was seeking something more creative. In an act of rebellion, I not only rejected banking but symbolically took my gold school ring to a shop and pawned it. I was slowly freeing myself.

In 1959, the three years over, graduation had arrived. My parents could not attend as Robin was graduating from Williams College the day before. They didn't see how they could be in two places at once. It was okay with me. I didn't like my school and would have happily skipped the whole thing. But it turned out to be a special occasion after all. First, because Robin did find a way to be in two places at once; he and his fiancée drove all night from Massachusetts to the southern border of Virginia just so they could clap for me when I got my diploma. That meant a lot. Second, we had the best graduation speech I've ever heard. It was delivered by one of the girls' fathers, the head of a publishing firm. As I remember, he said something to the effect: "This is a graduation speech you will never forget. I'm through. Good luck to you all!"

So on my very last day of school, two more events watered my spiritual whetting stone: I learned the powerful effect of a simple act of kindness (my brother's) and that brevity of words is more powerful than verbosity.

The naive 15-year-old who arrived at boarding school, left in 1959 a humbled, still fairly naive, 18-year-old, but with a mind sharpened with questions helping to cut through encircling walls. No longer would I complacently accept the unjust protection of privilege. My jackknife found new uses, this time to dissect cultural assumptions and reveal their inner workings.

A revered occupation which underwent my knife was that of fashion. Mother urged me to go to modeling school in a last ditch effort to make me more acceptable to society. One summer, I did go, traveling by bus from my home to Boston several times a week. There I was taught to be a social climber, dress only according to the rules of designers and to at all times strike a pose. It seemed a bit artificial and silly. On one trip home from this school of vanity, the bus rolled over on wet pavement, slid on its side down the highway, bounced upright against the median, then careened up an embankment. There were several injuries, but I was okay. I decided that was a sign and happily never returned to complete my schooling – not for the last time.

The summer following graduation, I took a job as assistant photographer at Mystic Seaport, a marine museum village. I boarded with an Italian family, socialized with everyone and had a dream of a time. Carrying a camera was my passport to unlimited access anywhere. I took many photos at this museum, learned to develop film and cataloged work for the Smithsonian. One time my boss and I were taken up in a two-seater plane to make aerial shots. He was tucked into the luggage area; I was given the passenger seat. I had been looking forward to this adventure; my first time on a plane, until I found the door on my side had been removed for a clearer field of vision to snap pictures. Suddenly, the pilot turned the plane on its side leaving me hanging in my seatbelt. I was so terrified that I dropped the heavy film slides straight down on the seaport full of people. Fortunately, nobody was hurt, but I was roundly reprimanded for such carelessness. I thought the pilot should have been reamed out instead.

I did not know at the time that my father had urged Mystic Seaport to hire me. The director there was later so pleased with my performance that he gave Dad a lifelong membership to the museum. My father never mentioned this to me, but eventually passed on the membership to my brother Henry, a serious boater. It was only quite recently, at age 76, that I accidentally found out about it. May some traditions be done with, such as the attitude of men that consider women unworthy of rewards.

Apparently, my boss did not make a report to his superiors about a terrible mistake I had made during my time working there. Maybe that was because it involved a project he should not have had me involved in while on the Seaport payroll. I was in the darkroom, developing wedding photos for a side job he had undertaken when, for some unexplainable reason, I suddenly threw on the electric switch, flooding the room with light. It was an unmitigated disaster, destroying every last romantic memorable picture of the bridal party. I stayed in there hiding out for an hour before finally opening the door and reporting what happened. Another humbling experience. The boss was hardly pleased, but could not very well report it.

That same year, I had promised I would submit to the debutante tradition. I felt I should at least do that for Mother before I struck out on my own in ways for which she would most likely not be enthused. My parents spent a lot of money on my fancy long white dress. They gave me parties and a ball. It meant a lot to Mother but it was unfortunately wasted on her ungrateful daughter. It made me neither more desirable nor elite.

Renegade at College

I had been accepted into the early admissions program at Smith College, persuaded by my aunt that I should go there. Finally, the rebel in me broke out: No, I did not want to walk in the societal path of righteousness. I preferred a country setting, a more prosaic place. Though not "ivy," Middlebury was considered a quality college. That is where I chose to go, expecting to be inspired by this honorable institution.

However, when I attended Middlebury, I was disappointed by its emphasis on earning good grades, preparing for the job world, speed reading, sports, sororities and fraternities. Unlike many others, my parents had not sent me to find a husband, having given up on that already, but to continue the process of lifelong learning.

I had gone to college hoping to discover new ways of thinking, to be challenged with fresh ideas – not to earn top grades, work toward a high-paying job, or cram piles of books into my brain. I found little of what I sought. Due to my privileged preparatory schooling, college, for me, was mostly a series of hum-drum repeat classes.

In English, we sped through quantities of classics in a few short weeks. I liked to read, but was this any way to treat great literature? Biology was boring lectures and labs, all of which I'd already taken – no exciting field trips, no research, no joy. The arts, however, were a different matter. There I was introduced to classical music, art history and painting. I have continued to take delight in all of these through the years.

Overall, however, I found the scene stultifying. I lived in a women's dormitory of double occupancy rooms. The first year I lived with a roommate who, in exasperation, took to repeatedly throwing a clock at my head. I was a bit too liberal for her. I requested a single room, but was told those were only for students with emotional or mental challenges. I tried to make the case that I qualified, but my plea fell on deaf ears.

My second year with a second roommate was more enjoyable. We had a housemother to protect us – from what I am not quite sure – but try to protect us she did. She was a gray-haired woman, a walking rule book. No phones, no pets, no guys, curfew at 11. What fun was that? I had a phone wired into the room, kept a pet squirrel, sneaked my boyfriends past the housemother, stayed out late and got regularly called into the dean's office.

I refused to be "rushed" for sororities – finding their candlelit rituals, secret oaths and cute blazers extremely silly. The dean berated me for refusing to play the game. "What is the matter with you," she asked. "Who are you to ignore these sacred traditions?"

"Why," the dean asked on another of my many mandatory visits to her esteemed office, "did you think a man could get away with using your college ID to get into a hockey game for free? He doesn't look remotely like you!" Because, I thought to myself, I have been loaning out my ID for almost two years and it has worked every time until now. After all, why should anyone pay to watch guys beat each other over the head in pursuit of a dumb hockey puck? But I stayed silent. Why blow a good thing? I continued to loan out my card.

One occasion found me hiding in a shower stall while the police raided the "frat" house in quest of girls, drugs and liquor. They found two out of three – but not me. Another time I absconded with a fraternity's secret red presidential robe, worn at its highly classified initiation ritual. Absurd as I thought their ceremonies, I found the robe to be quite nice: dark red with white trim, the fraternity insignia embroidered on the front and a hangman's hood attached. It made a great bathrobe and the hood was convenient for keeping my head warm after washing my hair. This act of "benign theft" as I liked to call it, did cause a slight stir. Late one night a swarm of motorcycles came roaring straight over the lawn up the hill to our dormitory – tough guys bent on revenge. As my roommate and I lived on the first floor, we were terrified. "Give them the robe, give them the robe!" my roommate screamed in panic. "I think that's what they want." Was she kidding, after all the work it had taken to get it in the first place, I wasn't about to give it up. But it ended well, at least for me. The police were called and, perhaps a bit unfairly, interceded before the guys managed to retrieve their holy grail. I wore that robe for many years.

Occasionally I took my blanket and pillow, had someone sign me in into the dorm, went out to a nearby field and slept under a watchful moon. The countryside was lovely. I had a boyfriend with a motorcycle and we traveled far and wide, the wind blowing my long hair out behind me (who knew about helmets?) and the sky alight with stars. We visited lakes, quarries, woods and fields. The mark of my college years was a constant open, draining wound on the inside of my calf from repeated contact with the bike's hot exhaust pipe.

One time a Volkswagen had been dismantled, snuck into our dorm and left outside my door. I don't remember why. Another time, a live goose was left there. I don't know what that was about either. The third time, it was a guy himself. That really got me in trouble. I was threatened with expulsion. He went back to his dorm, baked a chocolate cake, brought it to the housemother and charmed her into dropping the charges.

The year was 1961. "Tune in, turn on and drop out" pervaded the counterculture. So, after two years of having fun, but finding little inspiration in the rather conventional program, I opted to leave. My advisor was informed. "Why?" he asked, "Your grades are excellent. You are making a grave mistake. You need us to get a good job." Yes, there he was, confirming all I disliked: the fatherly patronizing authority figure talking down to me. And that was only the second time he had bothered talking to me since I had begun my studies there. I wanted to say, "Because of people like you." But I had already learned to smile and hide my feelings.

"I need to see the real world. I'm not finding it here in these ivory-towers," I proffered instead.

"Hah," he said, brimming over with a lack of understanding, "big mistake. You will never read a book again. You will become an ignorant American citizen."

"Why wouldn't I read? I consider reading a pleasure, not a chore. I am leaving so I can read with pleasure again," I remember responding to my advisor. What I really thought was that parents might have been impressed by a curriculum listing quantities of books covered in one semester, but I thought it a hoax. I was sent back to the dean's office. After two years of threatening to throw me out, she urged me to stay. Her words had little effect. The '60s were about rejection of the establishment. I left college.

One of the great thrills of my childhood summers had been the twice weekly visits to our local village library, a large stone building whose interior was lofty and quiet. Entering was like stepping into a church; I felt the same reverence. I loved the dim light and musty smell, never ceased to be amazed at the endless books full of adventure – there for me and me alone – just waiting to be picked out and taken home. Every night, after dinner, instead of talking, my parents and I sat reading for a couple of hours. Turning the pages, I traveled to new places, met new people, learned of foreign cultures and participated in wondrous adventures. Reading was rewarding and always continued to be.

Has life been easy without a degree? No. Should I have gone back at a later age? It might have helped me earn more money. Do I regret my decision? Not at all. What did I get from my college years? – A good introduction to the arts, and this story, of course, which for my parents was a rather expensive way to provide me with writing material.

CHAPTER 3

Overseas Education

"You're not going?" I asked in amazement. Together we'd planned a European trip. Now, at the last minute, my friend had backed out. Was her choice going to decide my future? No. So, 19 years old, though plenty anxious, I determined to go it alone. Of course, in those days traveling meant: no access to cell phones (or practically any phone), no internet, no email, nor Skype. When you bid the family farewell, it was final until your return. Nor did I carry a camera. It never occurred to me to take pictures. The only communication was through retrieving letters from American Express offices. Most large cities had them. There, mail for travelers was held until such time as it could be picked up. The world was a larger place back then: oceans wider, distances greater. Thus, cut off from friends and family, I would truly be on my own. I was to discover that traveling by one's self is the best way to immerse in a foreign culture.

I had told Dad I would work my way across Europe. Alarm bells went off. He must have been thinking things that had never occurred to me. He insisted on paying as he no longer needed the money for college tuition. In that case, wishing to be as little burden as possible, I decided to make the trip on a shoestring – and for the most part, I did. I sailed from New York on a Dutch liner. It took one glorious week to reach Europe. What a joy to watch dolphins leap through our wake; enchanting to stand on deck, absorbed by endless sky and sea; curious to be suspended between two worlds, frozen in time, neither here nor there.

Arriving in Paris, I spent my first couple of nights in a previously reserved room at a gracious Frenchwoman's home. However, her place was far from the center of Paris and I, eager to live in the hub, moved two days later to a tiny room above an Algerian nightclub. It was as cheap as I could find, short of sleeping on the street. This room had a narrow bed. That was it. A tiny window looked out on an airshaft. The bathroom down the hall consisted of a closet with a cement floor and two elevated foot rests upon which you squatted. When finished, you pulled the chain connected to a water tank overhead, then leapt for dry land as the water cascaded down, inundating the entire area. At night, I had to stand on the bed to make space to shut the door. After that, I'd lie there shaking to the wild beat of the African drums below until finally at 4 AM they ceased.

After a couple of sleepless weeks, I ran into friends I'd met on the boat. One was Peter Benchley who later wrote *Jaws*. He and I became quite close, deciding to share a room together with another guy. That lasted a week or more, until the two of them had a better idea – we could pool our money and rent an apartment. I could do the cleaning and cooking. Though women's lib was not yet in full stride, I nevertheless bristled at their condescension. "No way, not my style, not what I came to Paris for," I said to their astonishment. And so ended that "close relationship." I went searching for a new domicile.

I found it on the Left Bank, a tiny six-floor walk-up reached via a steep, narrow twisting, unlit staircase. For meals, I bought yogurt (first time I ever tasted it) or a baguette and liverwurst (first time for that, too), then brought them back to my room. This room held an iron bedstead, large armoire with a mirror on the front, tiny sink that on good days trickled mostly cold water, a small table, a chair and... no heat. The shared bathroom was two floors down. I loved the place. It felt just right. The concierge's 6-year-old daughter often visited me. I sketched pictures with her while she helped improve my French. It was like having family.

While living there, I discovered the writings of Simone de Beauvoir, who eventually became a leader in the French Women's Liberation Movement. Her thinking enthralled me. Here was someone to whom I could relate. Reading her autobiography, *The Prime of Life,* I was thrilled to learn that this famous woman I so admired, had most certainly lived in the very same room I now occupied. How perfect. No wonder it felt like home.

The center of Paris was everything I'd hoped for: handsome historic buildings, charming parks with winding walks, flowers, shade trees, nannies and children sailing model boats or playing on the grass. Streets were lined with cafés spilling tables and umbrellas onto sidewalks. There were museums galore, statues, monuments and every nationality of folks hurrying past. I enrolled at the *Alliance Francaise* to improve my French and found both a piano and art teacher to help my amateurish efforts. One evening I was practicing piano, while through the wall from the next room, a male quartet was belting out a rousing version of *Midnight in Moscow*. It was a glorious rendition, the first time I'd ever heard that magical song. It topped off my romance with Paris.

I met people from all over the world. Some of the men took me to Paris's famed opera house, or to concerts; one of my former professors took me to an elegant restaurant high up in the Eiffel Tower. We were served a gourmet meal and a flaming dessert while gazing out over the sparkling city. I met folks in cafés and in classes. I was privileged to hear a stirring *Messiah* concert in a historic cathedral filled with spires, sculptures and stained glass. Often I explored Paris alone, on foot, soaking in the feel of streets and people. I maintain that is the best way to discover a city's heartbeat.

Back then, discovering a new city was a far different adventure than it is today. There was no internet to Google for information on places to see, prices and schedules. Nor were there many guides to show you around, nor phones to call for help. We mostly depended on the famous Michelin Guides, a series of dark green booklets with tissue-thin pages, available for a number of European cities. Between the covers was amazing information about the histories, descriptions and locations of important places. I rarely left my room without one tucked under my arm. It made for exciting and challenging exploration.

Shortly after arriving in Paris, I made friends with a talented artist living in Montparnasse. She was lovely and, fortunately, short, as it had allowed her to escape from Hungary in her friend's suitcase when the Soviets invaded in 1956. She was fascinating and I learned much from her about keeping a positive outlook despite having suffered so much.

One evening, after visiting her, I hopped on the Metro to return home. At one particular stop, most folks got off. In fact, there was no one left seated ahead of me at all. I wondered why and looked out the window searching for clues. I saw none, but I noticed people on the platform looking back at me. I felt uneasy and wondered why they stared.

The train took off once more, rolled on for five minutes, slowed down, rounded a corner and came to a stop. We were not at a station. In the light from my car, I saw other trains next to us, all empty. Suddenly, the train's interior lights went out, the doors clicked and locked. The train and I had been bedded down for the night in an underground garage.

No need to panic, I told myself, no one can get to me, I'm shut up safely inside – unless, of course, someone is sitting behind me. And, if the lights are off, that means the heat is off as well. And what if I have to go to the bathroom, and what if they don't put this train back in action for another week? I lived by myself so no one would miss me.

Twenty minutes later, after talking myself down, I saw a shadowy figure in the distance, swinging a lantern. Solitude was less threatening than this. Oh please, I silently pleaded, please don't come this way. He came my way. When he was alongside the train, I ducked down so as not to be seen. No matter, he walked directly to my car, unlocked the door, climbed in, walked down to where I was crouching, hooked a long bony finger in my direction and ordered *"Venez!"* I "venezed" with him, too terrified not to.

We tramped down the aisle and out the door into the darkness, his lantern casting a faint glow. He led me in my long skirt and heels, across ribbons of tracks, frequently bending over, pointing and waving his arms back and forth while barking *"Non, non, non!"* I got it; those were the electrified third rails. He finally pointed me in the direction of steps leading up and out to the streets of Paris. It took me an hour to walk home. The lesson learned that night? Overconfidence could do me in. Pay attention to the locals. I realized I had much to learn, especially in a foreign country.

Parisians were intriguing. They could talk for hours, endlessly debating any subject at all. Cynicism was in high gear. No wonder, World War II had ended less than twenty years before. They had lived through a terrifying occupation, some participating in the underground, others colluding with the Germans. Some were sent to prison camps, others experienced shortages of food and streets full of tanks. History was no longer on the pages of a book, but alive and vivid. Compared to that, how privileged my own youth.

While I was there, in 1961, a conflict had kicked up. Soldiers with machine guns manned the street corners, the FLN (*Front de Libération Nationale*)[1] and the OAS (*Organisation de l'Armée Secrète*)[2] were fighting in Paris for dominance over Algeria. Streets were frequently closed due to bombings. I, the sheltered American, found this alarming. Parisians seemed to take it all in stride.

One day, I was in a large crowded elevator rising from a low level of the Metro to the street above. Suddenly the elevator stopped. Oh no – sabotage. How to escape? Were the other riders concerned? Not a bit. They divided into factions, taking positions on either side of the tight quarters and began arguing over who was responsible, the FLN or the OAS. "Whose side are you on?" they demanded.

Being the practical American, I replied, "I'm not on any side, I just want to find a way out of here, ring an emergency bell or climb out the top – something." Eventually, it turned out to be little more than a mechanical problem.

Another time, a huge explosion woke me. I lay frozen, waiting for what would follow. After a few minutes I heard voices on the street. Going to the French doors that opened from my room onto a tiny balcony, I saw Parisians in pajamas, carrying wine bottles, rush onto the street yelling, *"Bombe plastique! Bombe plastique!"* Someone had blown up an apartment in a nearby building. Everybody was drinking, talking,

---

[1] The party that had directed the Algerian war of independence against France (1954–62).

[2] A coalition of French middleclass colonists and patriotic segments of the French Colonial armed forces.

shouting and arguing about who had set it off. It was a macabre party. Debate: the Parisian approach to everything.

By good fortune, I was lucky enough to visit Les Halles, a place far more colorful than any artist ever splashed on canvas. One December morning, rising at 4 AM, I had taken the Metro to this famous central wholesale market of Paris. Massive iron and glass buildings, built in 1850, sheltered vendors supplying food for Parisian kitchens and restaurants. It was known as the "Belly of Paris."

I started my tour at the meat stalls. Streets were wet and glistening, gutters ran red with blood. Raw smells gagged me. Animals were strung up in their entirety – heads, bodies, legs and tails. Pig, cow, horse, boar and sheep heads stared vacantly. Butchers tossed hunks of meat back and forth without regard for customers in the flight paths. Beret-capped tradesmen raced four-wheeled carts up and down the aisles, forcing aside those in the way.

There were chickens, pheasants, ducks, geese and partridges, as well as boxes of tiny brightly feathered songbirds seeming too delicate to eat – all stretched out over several tables; gorgeous birds wickedly sacrificed to the gluttonous masses.

Vegetable stalls displayed orange carrots, brash red radishes, purple eggplants, yellow squash, multi-green lettuces and infinite shades of potatoes, all heaped in tottering piles. The odor of garlic was overpowering. Dripping ripe fruit in tropical colors were piled up, seemingly out of place on that gray, wet morning. Everything was to be sold by the end of the day.

Giant wheels of waxed cheese lined the many circling alleyways that spiraled around the marketplace; stacks and stacks in yellow, tan, brown and white oozing pungent odors. Thousands of eggs, yogurt cartons, bottles of milk, blocks of butter, baguettes, rolls, and loaves of bread loaded down the tables. Seafood stalls stretched on without end. Fish, stranded on ice, lay slick, glassy-eyed, their once vibrant colors faded to scaly grays and whites, their mouths gasping as if to say, "Throw me back, throw me back."

Laughter, shouting and swearing filled the air. From the rough, jolly Frenchmen came, *"Bonjour, Mademoiselle, ou-la-la!"* Paper, straw, feathers, bones and rubbish littered the ground. Trucks drove up and down the streets, up and down the walkways. Traffic jammed up, people yelled at each other, bikes and scooters navigated the chaos. Folks dashed about wrapped up in old hats, scarves, coats, blankets and shawls, anything to fend off the damp chill.

It was lucky I visited when I did. The lively Les Halles with all its *joie de vivre* was torn down in 1971 and relocated to the outskirts of Paris.

At Christmastime, I traveled to Mainz, Germany, where my cousin Margaret Holt and her husband were stationed. I had a lovely time with them, but what struck me the most were the stark, ugly new constructions interlaced with once beautiful bombed-out buildings. Massive WWII ruins were everywhere. In northern France, as well, I had seen the crumbling walls of houses and gardens still full of bullet holes – a sinister wakeup call for me. I began to understand how severe and widespread the atrocities of war, whether on the battlefront, in prison camps, concentration camps, gas chambers, or living under occupation. War is terrible. It changes people: some can never trust again, others are left eternally fearful. Parents become over overprotective. Many suffer lifelong poor health due to injuries or starvation. PTSD is as common to residents of occupied countries as it is to soldiers. A few have nervous breakdowns, even committing suicide. Faith is shattered. The idea that mankind is basically good becomes a cruel joke. The ripple effects carry down through generations. How lucky are those spared the insanity of war.

Returning to Paris, I stayed a few more weeks into January, but found it damp and chilly. A friend persuaded me that Italy, warmer and welcoming, was the place to be. So, with some regrets, I packed my bag and set off for Florence.

Italian Affair

Snugged down on the train to Florence, I awoke in the night to a brilliant star-filled sky, the moon-lit snowy Alps rising in ghostly peaks directly above me. I remained awake … enthralled.

Florence – city of elegance where an enlightened citizenry has preserved the finest historical art. Narrow streets meander through beautiful piazzas, basilicas, palazzos, ancient buildings and galleries with columned arches. Everywhere, both inside and out, fine statues, paintings and lively frescoes greet the visitor. It is a city of towers, spires, domed buildings and red-tiled roofs. The Arno River, coursing through the center of town, sparkles sunny and gay beneath the arches of the Ponte Vecchio with its colored stucco shops overhanging the water.

One day, while sitting in a café with an old school friend whom I chanced to meet in Europe, a couple of university students at the next table asked if they could practice their English with us. I had no problem with that as I found Italian men charming. One of them, a Northerner with brown hair and blue eyes, I found particularly likeable. He and I met at the café several times afterward before he asked me on a date.

Going out with him opened up a new world. He led me around Florence, pointing out astonishing architectural gems that, to my surprise, had not been mentioned in my famous Michelin guide. Our mutual interests in art and philosophy quickly bloomed into a mutual interest in each other. It was a torrid affair. Once he trusted that I was open to his culture, he introduced me to the life of the working class. His mother, who cooked for their family restaurant, fed us often. Hard as it was to make ends meet, her generosity was, nevertheless, unlimited. A large bowl of spaghetti was considered an appetizer. Meals were copious. "Eat, eat," she would tell me. I could never consume enough to satisfy her.

Saturday nights we gathered with other students at a table in the back room of a café. Drinks and food were beyond their means, but the generous owner allowed use of his space for free. We sat for hours, talking and laughing. I was impressed that lack of funds did not dampen spirits. I came to realize that it's not money, but attitude that allows one to enjoy such moments.

Working with his family at a vendor's booth in the Straw Market, I helped sell high-end leather pocketbooks to passing tourists. Because of my excellent grasp of English, tourists were impressed and bought more readily. I never let on. I also could never buy one of those expensive items. (Fifty years later, however, my thoughtful daughter, on a trip to Florence, was to purchase one and send it to me.)

My boyfriend took me to a camp in the northern part of Italy. There I saw more light-skinned, blue-eyed folks and a land of wooded mountains. It was quite different from the beautiful open Tuscan and Umbrian countryside with its vineyards, olive orchards and medieval walled towns. I had no idea that Italy's landscape was so varied, nor that all Italians were not dark-haired and olive-skinned.

A girlfriend and I spent ten days in Rome. While there, it turned cold and snowed, a rare occurrence. The concierge filled our hot water bottles every night as a heated room was not to be had. Because of the weather, beggars were desperate for money to purchase hot meals and the chance to sit in warm cafés. It was frightening to have men, women and children tearing at our clothes as we walked by. But, cruelly, we did walk by. Rome was a roaring metropolis, full of joy and despair. But, though I enjoyed the antiquity, extraordinary art and the ruins of the Coliseum, it did not hold the same charm as Florence.

One night we were chased back to our quarters by a mob of men on foot, scooters, motorcycles and bikes. Terrifying. We reached the safety of a hotel courtyard where we were able to close a large steel grille just in the nick of time. The guys made an unholy racquet yelling and pounding on the bars. Fortunately, someone called the police who arrived with sirens wailing and broke up the mob. However, they arrested nobody and found it all very amusing. Women seemed to be fair game in Italy.

I was anxious to visit Venice and went there next. It is a city of sun and crystal skies, cool air, people hurrying along sidewalks, gondolas gliding silently through canals and pigeons, thousands of pigeons. Here, immersed in water, foundered a city of glass and lace, elegance and wealth, of times past, a city sinking. Venice has sounds like no other city. One heard the click of heels on pavement, voices talking, birds singing, pigeons cooing and … no traffic.

I found personification of this romantic place in the refinement and grace of the gondolier: a man who knew his oar, his boat, every corner of every canal, the water and the sky. Gondoliers serviced the city. Some carried passengers; others were workers delivering merchandise such as milk, groceries and fuel. Even the Coca-Cola man was a gondolier. These men stood high on the stern of their boats, tilted their lean bodies forward, right foot behind left, perfect balance of tensions and sculled with a steady rhythm.

Canal men, whether dressed in raggedy black wool with scarves tied pirate fashion around their heads or dressed spiffily for tourists, fascinated me. Curious about their lifestyle, where they lived, how difficult their jobs were, I struck up a conversation with one of them, eager to learn more. I often sought him out when I needed a ride. One day, he invited me to join a group of his friends in a small hut by the Grand Canal. We nibbled fried food and I was given the honor of popping a Champagne cork to celebrate the purchase of a new gondola. Two glasses and two flower vases were filled and passed around for all to share. I, however, was given my own glass – true gallantry. They wound up the party by giving me a straw gondolier's hat enlivened with a gay red ribbon.

I had always wanted to ski in the Alps, so before winter passed completely, I set off for Austria. I promised my boyfriend I would be back, but in truth, our affair was beginning to fade. When I tearfully waved goodbye from the train, I think we both knew that the parting was final.

Northern Misadventures

I chose Innsbruck for my first crack at skiing the Alps. On day one, I skied in deep powder, something entirely new to me, challenging but wonderful. On day two, storms had moved in. A warning was issued: only experienced skiers should attempt the mountain. Cocky about my ability and not wanting to miss a single day of fun, I decided I fell into that category and set off for an early morning on the slopes. This irrational choice produced two frightening experiences.

The first came when the gondola (aerial this time), carrying twenty of us, stopped midway in the air halfway to the summit. One of the passengers explained it was probably because of high wind. "Like it might blow off the cable?" I asked.

"Hope not," was the less than reassuring answer. The car rocked violently, swaying back and forth; no operator aboard, no phone contact with anyone. We were high up above snow-covered cliffs and tiny toy trees – no rescue possible. I clutched the handrail.

"Won't help you much," someone snickered. We sweated it out for forty-five minutes. Then the car began once more to creep along, still swaying back and forth. "That's it," I said to myself and vowed never again to board such transportation.

Arriving at the top, I saw that the trail I'd followed down the day before was now roped off. Not knowing what to do and no English-speaking persons nearby, I opted to follow a group of skiers disappearing into a tunnel built to shelter from avalanches. I figured it would lead us around to another route. It did. We came out on a long slope on the other side of the mountain. Down we all whooshed. Fantastic. It was a wish come true until ten minutes later when we arrived, not at the bottom of the mountain, but in a ravine. All the skiers, I suddenly noticed, wore backpacks. They began unpacking and attaching climbing skins to their skis, then set off up the steep ascent of an impossibly tall peak.

Thus, my second regret. I had no skins, so attempted instead to clamber upward, herringbone style, through the deep snow. My heart sank when looking ahead, I saw the others climbing in a line, higher and higher, so far in the distance they appeared like a stream of ants on a mission. The scene reminded me of alpine skiers portrayed in a watercolor hanging on the other side of the world in my childhood home. Back then, I had never suspected that one day I would enter that picture.

I was exhausted, made little progress and finally, in despair, took off my skis and tried to walk – only to plunge up to my hips in the white fluff. Eventually, someone up ahead turned around and saw my dilemma. A skier was dispatched down the trail to see what the problem was. He fortunately spoke English. "Don't you have skins?" He asked in heavily-accented English.

"I didn't think I'd need them."

"Just where did you think you were going?"

"Around the mountain on a different trail to the bottom."

"Uh oh," he uttered. It turns out I had attached myself to an expert eight-person group: an Austrian backcountry ski team practicing for competition, both men and women, most in their twenties and thirties. To my chagrin, no one appeared the least bit tired. The trip would entail another six hours of climbing up and shushing down peaks across the top of the Alps. Only then would we ski to the bottom. Too late to go back. *What a dumb American I am*, was the first thought that came to me. The second was: *Not for one minute am I going to let them think I'm too wimpy to do this.* The next thought: *What if the high altitude gives me an asthma attack? They'll leave me here to freeze for clearly, once more, no rescue is possible.*

But survival demanded I put such ideas out of my head and focus on moving. My rescuer produced an extra pair of skins from his pack, helped me attach them and off we set together. When we caught up with the group, explanations were made. I saw a look of horror cross several faces. Then, on we climbed.

Fortunately, I was young, in pretty good shape and had skied since I was five. To my great relief, I was able to keep up, though I became increasingly tired. Once I tried to sit down and rest on a windswept rock sticking out of the snow. "Oh no," I was told, "no sitting on rocks. You'll never be able to have babies if you do that." Never have babies? Were they just afraid of letting me stop or did this Austrian team know something I did not? I stood up again. Some kind soul came to my rescue with several slugs of brandy.

We continued skiing across the roof of the world. The sky had cleared and the sun flashed brilliantly on distant snow-covered peaks, like the ones I'd seen weeks ago from the train window. This time, however, they were below, not above me. Further down, I could see dark conifers filling the ravines. An invigorating wind whipped my face, the snow sparkled, and the air was crisp. It was as close as I could be to heaven. In fact, I thought, maybe this is heaven. We're high enough. We clambered up peaks, then whooshed down, up and down, up and down for the next five hours. The view stayed with us, the sun continued to shine, I kept on drinking brandy.

Finally, we arrived at a hut dug into a snow covered slope. Inside, my ski mates started a wood stove and pulled out sandwiches that they generously shared with me. They were visibly relieved I had made it, though not nearly as relieved as I was. After lunch, we climbed bare rocks another 100 feet up. At the top, a black tin box was attached to a wooden cross. In the box was a notebook in which all who ever reached that point had signed their names. There weren't many. With great pride, I added mine.

Having rested, we left heaven and set off down the mountain. We flew down, down and down over wide open slopes, here and there jumping low snow covered rocks. I had never skied such a long descent before. It seemed like several hours before we reached the bottom. What a rush. "Where are we?" I asked when we arrived in an unfamiliar village.

"In Italy," they answered, "We'll take the train back to Innsbruck." Italy! I had brought neither passport nor money, thinking I would only ski a few runs, years ago at the beginning of this day. Once again, the team came to my rescue, paying for my train ticket and explaining to the border guards what a naïve American they had picked up by mistake; at least I imagined that is what they said. I couldn't understand their German but did not miss seeing the officials glance my way with a look of scorn.

That evening, I thanked my stars, and the Austrians, for my safe return to the hotel. Of course, fair play required I date one of my rescuers for a couple of nights. However, that fling was not to last. Remaining in Innsbruck was too expensive. I ran into a couple of travelers bumming around Europe. They shared a crazy secret with me: how to stay for very little money at an upscale resort in Zurs, one of the finest of ski areas. Their method for procuring cheap quarters sounded farfetched. Nevertheless I was game to try so packed up and moved on again.

Sneaking in the Back Way

I traveled by bus up, up and up to the picturesque village of Zurs tucked high in the Alps of Austria. We drove through a long dark tunnel: road protection from avalanches. On arrival, I made my way to the recommended resort. When all the other guests finished checking in, I summoned my courage and approached the desk. "Can I rent your bathroom?" I asked, a little nervously.

"The bathroom?" answered the clerk, peering down his nose with a look of disdain. "We rent bedrooms, not bathrooms. Why would you ever ask such a thing?"

"Because another traveler told me that you do."

He hemmed and hawed, then allowed they had done it on occasion if the guest really had no money. "That would be me," I said, relieved my informants had not totally misled me into making a fool of myself. He brought me upstairs to the bathroom – a room with several tubs, no showers. If you wanted a bath, it had to be in a tub. If you needed toilet facilities, they were in a separate room. Private bathrooms were unheard of.

A narrow locker was provided in which to stuff my bag. The staff would set up a cot between the tubs where I could sleep but not until after midnight. I had to be out of there before 6 AM. I was free to enjoy the rest of the resort, including the great room, a dining room and game room. All meals were included in the price. And the price? A quarter of the going rate. What a bargain. It had worked.

I stayed there for a week, skiing my heart out on the wide open, deep powder slopes. For some, it takes more than one mistake to wise up. That was me. One day, at the top of a mountain, I took a wrong trail and found myself at dusk in the town of Lech, once more without money for transportation back to the resort. I set out on the long walk back following a road in the dark, skis over my shoulder. Suddenly, I heard an avalanche come sweeping by, sounding like a train and too close for comfort. I fervently prayed I was not in its path. A little later, after several efforts at thumbing a ride, a couple stopped and gave me a lift to Zurs but not without first lecturing me on the dangers of hitchhiking. I agreed wholeheartedly and promised myself never to ski without cash again.

After a week in Zurs, I was ready to leave but had to cancel my plans. Avalanches had been sliding over the only road out closing it off for several days. When finally it cleared, I took a leap of faith, assumed it was now safe, and boarded the first bus out. We made it in good shape.

What next? Spring was slowly traveling north. I'd heard Holland was the place to best meet up with it. Off I set for the Netherlands where if I thought I'd already had some pretty life-changing experiences, none of them compared to what was to come.

CHAPTER 4

Upheaval

Arriving in Amsterdam, I made my way to the youth hostel to secure a bed for the night. "Better get in early," I was advised by a fellow traveler, "They oversell the beds. He who arrives last has no place to sleep." It was Easter time and tourists had flocked to Holland to see the lush flowers bursting forth in gardens and fields. The dormitory style room was packed full. I found myself a bed and, following advice, turned in early.

Several hours later I was awakened by a voice proclaiming, "Someone's in my bed!" I lay very still, pretending to sleep. Eventually, the voice went away. How cutthroat I'd become. Not an admirable quality. I'd better watch that, I told myself, best to leave for a quieter place. So the next day, after walking around the gorgeous city of Amsterdam filled with canals, houseboats, and ancient stepped gabled houses,[3] I took a train to Enkhuizen, some 60 kilometers north of Amsterdam. The guidebooks had described this as a small outlying city on a harbor of the inland sea of Holland, referred to at that time as the Zuiderzee.[4] We passed field after field of brilliant tulips – one red, the next yellow, another white; some fields dressed in bright green with black and white cows and sheep dotting the landscape. Ditches and canals crisscrossed the colored squares. The sun poured down, saturating the scene.

Enkhuizen was all the guidebooks had promised – and more: few tourists; fishing boats filling the harbor; narrow cobbled streets; little traffic; outdoor cafés and masses of brilliant flowers by every home and on every spare piece of ground. It was a fairytale kind of place. I fell in love with it at once.

I rented a bike, the common mode of transportation, rode out into the rural areas where white farmhouses with red-shutters and tall thatch roofs nestled in tulip fields and grass pastures. A hotel employee offered to

[3]Stepped gables refer to the architectural feature of buildings whose gables are shaped like a staircase going up both sides to a squared-off peak.
[4]A large dike, (Afsluitdijk) built in 1932, closed off the Zuiderzee (South Sea) from the North Sea. Water levels dropped and polders, arable swaths of reclaimed land diked in on the sea bottom, were created. The remaining water became known as the Ijsselmeer and constitutes the largest lake in Western Europe.

show me an old fortress called De Drommedaris: or De Drom for short. Rising by the harbor, it stood tall and forbidding. He knocked on an ancient wooden door that swung open – to an amazing new chapter of my life.

American Maid in Enkhuizen

Knock on De Drom's* door.
Knock on the past,
tap on the future.
Worn wood, tired hinges
creak open to a half-lit room,
first floor of a tower
built 1540,
on the shores of the
Zuiderzee, once harbor guard
for the Dutch East Indies
mighty trading firm.

Hesitant, I step inside.
Arches soar above,
scattered tables
line the curved brick walls,
bar and kitchen to one side.
Chopin and Schubert
fill the magical space,
As a fellow sits a trash can,
foot thumping,
fingers running the keys
of an old upright,
a scene I oft recall,
even now, some fifty years on.

Enchanted American,
I stayed, worked,
lived in this ancient tower.
One day, opening a door
I was startled by black water
filling the staircase,
entrance to an old
tunnel leading
to the village gate,

flooded, history-drowned.
A great wing enlarged the tower,
arched the road
to a drawbridge.

Once a fortification
and a prison,
then reborn
a center of culture,
this fortress by the sea
rose three stories high,
walled deck and turret on top,
from which, in former times,
crow's nest threat at sea to spy.
Today, a tourist lookout
to spy on red tiled roofs,
narrow winding streets,
and, on silky moonlit nights
fishing boats at sea.

My sleeping room,
an eight by ten old prison cell
behind thick double-doors,
short, narrow, pierced by
small windows
through which food,
meager no doubt,
was passed centuries ago
to poor locked-up wretches
whose only view,
broken by bars
sunk deep into the bricks,
faced nothing but sky.
Lurking about,
ghosts of men
whose prayers
inscribed in the
low wood-vault ceiling
still haunted the room.
I was young then, slept well,
dreamt of bygone days,
of battles and victories,

of great feasts served
in the hall below.

We hosted artists, musicians,
tourists, held exhibits,
concerts, pipe smoking contests.
(Who could puff a meerschaum the longest?)**
We drank our share of cognac,
played chess deep into the night.

And oh the stories from those days.
How we used a pulley,
lifting each course in a basket
through a trap door
from kitchen to upstairs diners,
just as soldiers once hauled
ammunition to gunners.
The coffee pot tipping, spraying
all below in a hot brown shower.

The sweaty tired baker who,
there for bread delivery,
tried helping with the
mashed potatoes.
The masher broke,
into the trough he fell,
salting the mash for all to tell.

Three AM walks by the harbor to see
the brown, square-sailed fleet come in,
unload its catch,
fish packed off to market
midst shouts, the rumble of wheels,
and rattle of rigging.

Flying over the ice to Urk,
wooden skates strapped to our boots,
far from shore lights,
boom of ice for music,
moon showing the way.

Those were good times,

in that castle by the sea.
Cherished memories
held close through the years.
And the piano player?
What became of the chap?
Willem Tissot was his name.
I listened well and married him.
How could I not?
A wedding dinner in the tower
brought good cheer
To love's magic power.

*De Drom is the nickname for De Drommedaris, a 16th century fortification built on the shores of what used to be called the Zuiderzee, great inland sea of the Netherlands.

**Meerschaum refers to a pipe made of material of this name and said to be so fine it lifted smoking to an art form. The material is a hydrous magnesium silicate composed of tiny fossilized crushed seashells.

But how did our courtship begin? – when Wim took me, sitting sidesaddle on a luggage rack on the back of his bike, for a 25-mile trip to visit his parents. The Dutch can do everything imaginable on their bikes. After a few months' long courtship, we announced our engagement to his family. His mother fled to the garden in tears, his father refused to give his permission to marry[5] and his grandfather pounded the table, declaring he would not have the family bloodline tainted by a foreigner. It was a curious statement for a man who was married to a short, slant-eyed, brown-skinned Indonesian wife. "What about her?" I wanted to ask but held my tongue. Nevertheless, Wim and I persevered with plans. His family feared he was marrying beneath his position, mine feared I was marrying beneath mine. Eventually, after a bumpy start, everyone came around.

We were married a short six months later. My parents, my brother Henry and his wife Anne came from America to celebrate. Wim's parents refused to attend the pre-wedding dinner in De Drommedaris, heartily disapproving of our "radical" friends who gifted us the evening. The night before marrying I thought maybe I should try on my wedding dress. It was a pink lace sheath that had been my mother's when she was married. Alas, it was too small; I was a bit chubby in those days. My heroic mother sat up most of the night letting it out so I could slip into it

---

[5]In the Netherlands, in 1962, anyone up to the age of 25 who wanted to marry had to have signed permissions from both parents.

with ease. My parents also treated me to an appointment with an expensive hair stylist. He worked an hour to make me presentable. Horrified at the result, I immediately washed away the expensive "do". It was back to straight hair for me.

The wedding ceremony was held at the historic town hall in Hilversum. Fortunately both families attended. The official in charge was required to deliver the vows in two languages. After he laboriously bumbled through the English part, Wim spoke up to say we had all gotten the idea and would prefer not sitting through it again in Dutch. That was followed by an awkward silence during which the official ended the ceremony and promptly left, forgetting to have us sign the wedding license. From the town hall we drove to a rustic restaurant for the reception. We had hired a pianist who played a few tunes then disappeared. Upon asking where he went, we learned Wim's mother had fired him, worried her in-laws would be shocked at the jazzy music being played on such a solemn occasion. We actually thought we were there to celebrate so Wim hopped on a bike, rode to the man's house and hired him back.

Prior to our wedding, we had moved to a single room on Amsterdam's Nieuwe Prinsengracht (a canal in the center of the city), sharing the kitchen and toilet facilities with the folks next to us. The kitchen consisted of two gas burners, one sink and no refrigerator. I learned much about preserving food without cooling, shopping the open market, and Dutch cooking. As Holland was to be my new home, I also bought workbooks and taught myself the language. It was fun learning the grammar, words and sounds. Taking up residence in a new country was an exciting adventure.

In the adjacent room lived a prostitute and her Surinam boyfriend. At least every other night these two would get into violent fights. The landlord would run down from upstairs, call for Wim, and together they would try to prevent the guy from killing his "sweetheart." Separately, these two neighbors were nice, but the combination was explosive.

The stress of not sleeping due to the constant nightly violence next door caused an outbreak of my old childhood problem: eczema. From an early age, I used to bloody the sheets every night from scratching at my constantly burning and itching skin. It seemed an insolvable problem until Mother found a man who was not officially qualified, in fact considered a quack, but had purportedly helped in similar cases. When I was 7 years old, he prescribed a sticky coal tar ointment which he made himself. I had to smear it over my legs, torso and arms. Mother sewed long-legged cotton pants (strange for a young girl in those days of dresses only) and long-sleeved shirts to cover the ointment and not irritate my skin. The smell was terrific, similar to that of the hot tar used to pave roads. It was an isolating ordeal, leaving me with few friends. It took a year of treatment but in the end, I was cured. I remained eczema free until the outbreak experienced in Amsterdam. There, I became so sick from the rash that I couldn't sleep and missed a couple of weeks of work. This was my first introduction to how a socialized country functions. The doctor visits, prescribed medicines and all missed days at my job were paid in full.[6]

Mother had shipped over my cocktail dresses from an earlier time, little aware of the 180^0 turn my life had taken. Not needing such attire, in fact now finding the fashion ridiculous, I thought the prostitute might enjoy dressing up American style, so gave the clothes to her. She did. We often saw her nights, modeling them quite nicely on the street corners. The clothes proved a distinct business asset.

Our landlady was determined to reform the prostitute and her lover. She would not evict them. The lack of sleep caused by the chaos next door finally became too much, and we moved again. Housing was scarce in those postwar years, due primarily to the baby boom. To find an affordable apartment, one went on a waiting list. It could take up to two years before something in the desired vicinity became available. Rather than waiting, we had found our room on the black market. The downside: it cost the same as what Wim's parents paid to rent an entire house and yard. So, where to go next?

·

---

[6]Years later I was to buy a patented over-the-counter ointment for a repeat but mild outbreak of eczema. It smelled just like the ointment I had used as a child and in fact, had most of the same ingredients that my "quack doctor" had first discovered. It was a reminder that just because someone is not officially qualified, does not mean their discoveries are without merit.

CHAPTER 5

Hiding in Plain Sight

Wim had often ridden his bike the 9 kilometers from Amsterdam to the village of Ouderkerk, frequently stopping at a wonderful tavern called "Het Jagershuis" (tavern by the towpath). It was there he learned that the owner had a row of condemned fishermen's houses on the adjoining property. The landlord, Mijnheer Brouwer, anxious to make a few guilders, offered to rent us one until we moved again or the houses were torn down.

This lovely stucco house, stained with age and sporting a mossy, orange tiled roof and crooked wooden door, was to become one of my favorite homes ever. We had a kitchen (though still no refrigerator), a living room and bedroom, all with cracked yellowed walls and slanted floors. Bricks propped under legs of our furniture kept everything more or less level. It was charming.

There was but one working toilet located at the far end of the row of connected empty houses. To reach it, we walked outside to the farthest door and made our way in the dark through several abandoned rooms. Unfortunately the toilet was right under a boarded up window with a sign tacked on the outside announcing the houses were condemned. Before flushing, we had to determine whether anyone was passing by on the sidewalk who might give us away.

Our small backyard edged the Amstel River; in fact, the house and the yard were *below* the level of the river. In this tiny yard were flowers, apple trees and a lovely shaded bench. The Amstel, not 40 feet from the house, carried an endless parade of impressive barges churning downriver. The captains' families lived on these boats that often flew a line of colorful wash above their decks, flower gardens in tubs and children waving from playpens. The comforting chug-chug of the passing barges shook the ground as well as our house, which was built without foundations on ground consisting of peat. Every other day we took our baskets and walked to the hand operated ferry that ran via a cable across the Amstel. On the other side we bought our groceries from shops lining the main street: the baker, greengrocer, fish market and butcher.

One night, 10 miles down the road, an ammunition factory exploded. Our house, with us in it, rose up, seemed to hover in the air, then settled again. We breathed a sigh of relief for we had grown attached to our unauthorized home.

41

While in Holland, I worked for an office of Time-Life Inc. Wim worked for Wagon-Lits Cook Travel Agency. Generous wedding gifts had come from America in the form of money. After working for several months, already contemplating a trip to the U.S., we made the crazy decision to give up our jobs, live off the presents and enjoy the countryside and culture. We biked, skated the canals, took in foreign films and had an extraordinarily good time. Something we have never regretted doing.

After we'd been married a year, my parents offered us a trip to the States. Wim declared, "If I have a chance to visit America, I don't want to stay for only two weeks. I'll get a job so we can remain twelve months."

Ouderkerk gave us a rousing sendoff in the adjacent tavern with the landlord, a talented musician, cranking out music on his accordion. Leaving brought mixed emotions. I found the entire country, urban and rural, unusually beautiful. But the numerous laws and social conventions were constricting: how the outside of your house should be maintained, which day one did the wash, when one shopped, what to serve for supper, how often to wash your sidewalk and in certain villages, no biking on Sundays. In fact, some villagers still threw stones at Sunday bikers. The list went on and on. Only later did I realize that this implicit civic obedience went a long way toward ensuring relative harmony in an overcrowded country. Life in the cities, on the other hand was, and still is today, far more liberal and lively.

Living in the Netherlands was my first exposure to the notion that unregulated capitalism and the pursuit of profit do not produce the best outcome. There, the heavily taxed population readily accepted the belief that government was there to help *all* citizens to a decent living, not just the wealthiest: no one suffered from lack of healthcare, housing or food. A disciplined community meant a thriving country. For the most part, it is still that way today. There were, and still are few objections to this humanitarian approach, even from those who pay the largest share.[7] America could learn something from this.

---

[7] Unfortunately, today, the concept of privatization has crept into government; trains and the postal service have been privatized. As a result, neither works very well anymore.

CHAPTER 6

Taking Stock – New Ventures

We arrived in America in August, 1963, first visiting my parents for two weeks. I began reflecting on my European life and how it had affected my perceptions of the world. There, history had come alive as it never had in school. I began to understand how vast the planet, how insular America, how diverse other cultures, and how no one single country has all the answers.

Visiting bombed-out and bullet-strafed villages in central Europe, I became vividly aware of how recently WWII had taken place and the dreadful mess it had made of innocent lives, not only for those killed but far into the future for those who survived. Until then, war had been something learned only from books and movies.

My eyes were also opened to the countless different ways folks in Europe live out their lives, all as valid as mine. Did they want to move to America as I had so often been told? They did not then and they do not now. Our way is not the only way. And finally, I learned to bow to other customs, not be afraid to ask questions and take responsibility for my own actions.

After staying with my parents, we moved to a newly founded boarding school in Stowe, VT. From overseas, Wim had been hired to teach French and Latin. The students consisted, in large part, of delinquent kids from wealthy homes: a rough crowd for a foreign rookie teacher. At various times over that first year, the students managed to light the school on fire, loosen the bolts on the school bus so the wheels would fall off, run an active cocaine ring, regularly knock holes in the walls and practice archery and knife throwing in the halls. "I'm not crazy about teaching in America," Wim muttered. I assured him it was not like this everywhere. We stayed a year during which the math teacher punched out the headmaster; the religious teacher ran away with another headmaster's wife; a number of teachers quit before the year was half over; and I gave birth to our son Christopher.

Just before my due date, we were moved to a slightly larger apartment in one of the dormitories where a pet monkey had been allowed to run free in what was to be our son's nursery. I spent the last month before his birth, washing, scrubbing and repainting the "cage" room, extremely worried about stray germs lurking in corners and ready to pounce. As soon as I finished, the headmaster decided our apartment was nicer than his, and we had to move again, this time to a girls' dormitory.

The only doctor in town was nicknamed Bones. He made a good living caring for wealthy skiers who traveled from the city to break legs and arms on Mount Mansfield's ski slopes. There was a picture of a crutch crossed with a ski inlaid on his waiting room floor. "If it's between delivering your baby or attending to an accident," he warned, "you will be on your own." Fortunately it was icy that day; the slopes were closed.

Christopher was born in February, 1964, black-haired and sturdy. At first he seemed well, but constant crying alerted me that something was wrong. "You're just a nervous mother," declared the doctor in a condescending tone. Indeed I was, and with good reason. The problem was finally discovered: he had an intolerance to breast milk as well as most substitutes. His digestive track ripped open, and thus weakened he developed pneumonia. This meant several admissions to what was then called Mary Fletcher Hospital in Burlington, VT. Care was excellent. On each visit, we found, to our relief, that the nurses were carrying him around as if he was their own. Strangely, he was eventually cured by putting him on a formula made of meat. After four months in and out of the hospital, he finally recovered and we got to bring him home for keeps.

One day, exhausted from those previous months of tension and worry over our baby, Wim suggested we get a sitter and take an evening away. We drove two hours north to hear Thelonious Monk play in Montreal. For the 2 AM return, I was the designated driver. Wim and the two teachers with us had to be ready for morning classes and so fell asleep. I was cruising along, doing 60, when lights flashed by on either side of the car. I'd blown straight through customs. Terrified the officers would start shooting, I speeded up to escape, only to find the road ahead blocked by a barrier. To avoid it, I took a sharp turn on two wheels. That got the attention of my passengers. "What's happening?" they bellowed.

"Heads down," I yelled to their astonishment, "They may try to shoot." Luckily, they did not. We raced into Vermont at 80 mph. Were the customs officers asleep? Would they really have shot at us? Today? Yes. Back then? I doubt it. That was the last time those teachers traveled with us.

CHAPTER 7

City Life

Wim claimed he had never decided to move to America; he just hadn't decided when to return to Holland. That was over fifty years ago. The truth was: the longer he lived here, the more impressed he was by the way American children grew up with a sense of self-confidence and enterprise, something lacking in his own upbringing. Childrearing in the Netherlands, he observed, was more constricting, timid and overly disciplined. He had grown up in a world full of fear and suffering due to the hardship and aftermath of the German occupation. It would take its toll on his generation and generations to come. War is never over when it's over.

In June, we moved to a third floor walk-up in Hartford, CT. It was not modern but spacious. Wim took a job as a French teacher at Kingswood Academy, a private day school modeled after its namesake in Bath, England. There he met a history teacher, Jim Goodwin of Adirondack fame. Little did we imagine that one day we would end up living in the wilderness park where Jim had pioneered as a guide and crafted new trails.

Kingswood School was in many ways opposite from Stowe Prep. The teachers had only recently given up wearing long black gowns. The school was all white and tightly run. Jewish boys had been admitted for the first time only the previous year.

At the same time as teaching, Wim applied to the French literature MA program at Trinity College but did not have a BA from the University of Amsterdam, a requirement to begin working on his master's degree. In those days, Dutch universities awarded no other degree than a PhD. Trinity asked Wim to get written proof that he had completed all the required undergraduate work. He went to great lengths to obtain the necessary documents. When they finally arrived from Holland, Trinity administrators said, "Now please translate, we can't read Dutch." The point of it all? He was accepted into the program, studied nights and graduated three years later with a Master's degree in French Literature.

Christopher, just four months old when we moved to Hartford, began to thrive despite his early troubles. One evening, we treated ourselves to a night out. We left our precious baby with a highly recommended sitter, an older German woman whose English was just passable. "If he cries and

45

won't settle down," we told her, "just soak a washcloth and let him suck on it. He'll fall asleep in no time." On returning home, we were greeted by a distraught woman.

"I *soaped* the cloth like you tell me but he just cry and cry all the evening," she declared in amazement.

Soap was to play another role in my life. One day I made vichyssoise from a can of potato soup and poured it into a pitcher to be ready for supper. Then I thought I should taste it first, so I took a swig from what was left in the blender. It was dreadfully bitter. Oh no, botulism! Christopher was napping. I called my neighbor and told him what happened. "I'm going to unlock the front door, then lie down for a while. Please check on me in a half-hour and call an ambulance if needed." Afraid I might die but hoping it was a less lethal bacterium, I drank several gulps of mustard and hot water in an effort to throw it all up. Then I really got sick. Oh to leave my child when he was so young and forsake my beloved husband too. I lay down for a while, feeling awful until I remembered I had squirted Ivory Soap into the blender after dumping out the soup. It was the Ivory Soap I drank, not the soup, and it was the Ivory Soap, the mustard and the hot water that made me so ill.

It was in Hartford, in 1966, that our daughter Martha was born. I had had a difficult time when in labor with Christopher and determined the next experience would be different. Searching through a number of books, I came upon one describing the Lamaze method. I studied it closely, practicing all the exercises and breathing techniques. When I went into labor with Martha, it went smoothly. At that time, Lamaze was a new and little known approach for coping with contractions. The nurses were impressed. They had never before heard of it.

Tiny and fragile, three weeks premature, Martha quickly developed into an energetic and mischievous playmate for her brother. A neighboring interracial couple, Lloyd and Bobbi, lived in the apartment across the hall. We became good friends. Their two children played with Christopher and Martha almost every day. He was an African-American musician, often out performing gigs until late at night. We spent many evenings visiting with Bobbi while waiting for him to come home so we could party together.

Wim, curious about American working class people and their culture, liked to hang out in coffee shops. They were both affordable and offered a good cross-section of American life. One day he eagerly invited 4-year-old Christopher and me to join him at a "fascinating" place he'd discovered. He took us to a coffee house for transients and the homeless located under the tracks in downtown Hartford. It was a sad collection of a misguided culture's rejects. Here bad coffee was served in thick white china cups. When Wim and I returned to our table with a tray of food, we found

Christopher sitting in the corner twitching, his head jerking, arms twisted, his eyes rolling. "What's the matter?" we asked in alarm.

"Nothing," he said, "I'm just doing what all these other people do."

He was an observant child from the start, imaginative too. One night, he began crying out after we put him to bed. We had left a nightlight on and the door open. "I'm afraid," he cried.

"What of?" we said. "We left the door open and we're right here."

"No, no," he sobbed, "Shut the door. I don't want the monsters to get out!" Evidently those monsters were an integral part of his comfort zone.

I was determined to give our children the best start possible. I had read about a program for teaching children to read at the young age of eighteen months. I ordered all the prescribed large letter cards and tried to get Christopher interested – to no avail. Finally, I shoved them under the bed and forgot about the material until a year later. Christopher crawled under our bed to reappear covered in dust and dragging the non-illustrated word cards. One by one he looked at them and asked, "Why does this say father? Why does this say mother? Why does this say car?" Astonishing. Maybe there was some validity to the early learning theory after all.

While I felt privileged and happy to be at home with the children, I was always reaching out for a little more. I attended evening classes in the Greek classics, did some painting (setting an easel in the bathtub for lack of space), practiced the piano and experimented with cooking and sewing (most projects ending up in the trash). I excelled at little but still thought it important that children learn adulthood has its own pleasures, that life has meaning beyond parenting and that there are good reasons to want to grow up.

CHAPTER 8

Seeking a New Path

Because Wim was planning to study for his doctorate, my parents generously offered us their guest cabin, close to where they now lived on Brooks Pond in Spencer, MA. Earlier, while I was still in boarding school, Mother and Dad had sold our city house and Dad remodeled The Barn into their year round-home. Dad then converted the cabin to a three bedroom house to accommodate our using it. There we could live rent-free while Wim carried on his studies. So, after three years, we moved again. On moving day, I went ahead with the kids. Wim stayed behind to load the U-Haul, a couple of friends helping.

After settling into our new quarters, Wim began his doctoral studies at the University of Massachusetts, Amherst. He also worked to support us by teaching undergraduate students in Boston at Boston University, Regis College, Assumption College and graduate students at St. Hyacinth's College and Seminary. It required an enormous amount of commuting and preparation.

Some weeks after we first moved, I began to notice things missing. On asking Wim about it, he replied, "When we finished packing the apartment, it seemed we had more than enough for one family, so I just left everything in the storage room behind." Once over my shock, I started thinking about that. He was right. We did have way too much stuff. From then on, I viewed every move as a way of taking a closer look at how much we really needed and an opportunity to donate the rest to charity.

We invited our good friends Lloyd, Bobbi and the children to visit our new home. I was embarrassed at my parents' polite but shocked reaction to this interracial family. I was disappointed with myself for worrying about this. When the day came that I no longer worried about the opinion of family and friends, I felt I would be truly liberated from racism. However, it took five years. How hard it is to overcome inbred attitudes.

To help with the budget, I took a part-time job as an aide in a nursing home. Understaffing and poor care were appalling. After two nights of orientation on the 3-11 PM shifts, I was left in charge of thirty patients to care for by myself. One of the patients was dying with no family or friends at his bedside. Between the impossible task of offering care to all the others, I would stop by his room and try my best to keep him cleaned up and comforted. It was heartbreaking. About 10 PM, I was at his side when he looked up at me and said, "Don't worry, you'll get yours too," rolled over and died. A tough moment. I had tried my best, but staffing was short and there was only so much I could do. It started me thinking about how we treat our elderly. Now, some forty-five years later, I don't see much improvement. If you are wealthy, no worry; if not, Heaven help you.

It was during this time in Massachusetts that my mother and I took an evening course in pottery. I fell in love with the craft and was hooked. I set up a studio in the basement and threw pots whenever I had a free moment. Readymade glazes were available but expensive and only came in small jars. Interested in making rather than buying them, I took a short glaze course and quickly found myself plunged into chemistry and physics. Continuing to study on my own, I became increasingly fascinated by the exciting results when combinations of minerals were exposed to the mystery of fire. Opening the kiln each time was like Christmas morning – full of surprises.

The cabin was on a pristine lake near my parents' home. Set upon a small hill on a private peninsular, the location was unrivaled for beauty. The children learned to swim, paddle, and explore the woods. Summers we could drive to our house. Winters we could not. While we loved skating on the pond and sliding down the hill on which our house sat, access was difficult. There was a garage down at the end of our long driveway. We wore snowshoes and had to sled in groceries and children. This worked well until the day Martha became sick, spiking a 103^0 temperature. I called the doctor to ask him to prescribe an antibiotic. My mother would drive the 4 miles to town and pick it up. He insisted I bring Martha to his office. I explained that that would involve first pulling her in a sled for a quarter of a mile with a hard wind blowing and the thermometer hovering at 10^0, then tucking her into a frigid car for the long ride to his office. "It will be good for her," he replied, "bring that temperature down." And so I brought her in and he was right. After that bitterly cold trip, her temperature dropped right back to normal.

The challenging access presented another problem: what to do with the garbage. I tried sledding it out, tucked in beside Martha, but it continually fell off the toboggan and scattered over the hillside. The solution was to store it in the woodshed where it could remain nicely frozen until spring came. However, the days started to warm and the garbage thawed before the road. When the road finally opened and I began to move the mess into our station wagon, it came alive with rodents. The black bags writhed and burst open, gray furry things exploding out in every direction. I loaded the car, then put Martha in the car seat in front with her snowsuit on and hood pulled up. I pulled up my hood as well. Christopher stood on the front seat facing backward. I gave him a bat and told him to hit anything that moved. For 5 miles I cringed behind the wheel and listened to whack, whack, whack as he gleefully slammed into the seething mass. The ultimate game of Whack-a-Mole!

The children often stayed with my parents. One evening, there was a cocktail party. Christopher was wandering about among the guests when suddenly the outdoor lights, shining on the surrounding lawn and woods, went off. Walking up to the plate glass window and peering out into the black night, he proclaimed, "Darkness there and nothing more, quoth the raven, Nevermore." We had often listened to recordings of Poe's poetry and Christopher, at age five, with impeccable timing, put his knowledge to use at just the right moment. Did he ever make my parents proud.

Our kids developed a strong bond with their grandparents. It was an idyllic setting for both sides of the sandwich. However, the filling (that would be Wim and me), did not fare so well. My opinions were often in conflict with those of my parents. They believed in white superiority; that folks were poor because they didn't behave; that there was but one acceptable lifestyle; that heritage mattered; that privilege was deserved. Already, back in 1952, I had begun to have my doubts about their views when listening with my mother to the radio during the McCarthy era as the House un-American Activities Committee went after numbers of prominent people. I did not know who most of them were. However, when they accused the wonderful Pete Seeger and Charlie Chaplin of being anti-American criminals, which my parents believed, I could not accept those views. I was often torn both then and later – loving my parents but rejecting many of their values. Wim, my delightfully socialist husband, would really get my father steaming. I asked him to please not bring up politics when visiting, but he just couldn't resist. One day at Sunday dinner, he turned to my father and said "Pretty exciting to see all LBJ's (Lyndon B Johnson) programs taking effect." There was a long tense silence before Dad turned to him and said,

"Nice try Wim."

My father, Rodney Washburn, an arch-conservative and like his own father, president of the Mechanics National Bank of Worcester, was a respected member of the community. I was but Rodney's daughter. I needed to distance myself from him. I had no substance. As for Wim, the demands of long commutes, home life, work and study in what proved to be a very dry program all became too much. In 1968, like the gypsies we were, we packed up and moved again, this time to Bennington, VT. Wim found work teaching at nearby North Adams State College in North Adams, MA (Later to become Massachusetts College of Liberal Arts).

CHAPTER 9

Rocking the '60s

Since North Adams (a run-down factory town) looked too unattractive to raise a family in, we rented a house beside a river on Main Street in Bennington, VT. In fact, one wall of our house stood *in* the river. Every night during the spring, I would get up a couple of times to look down at the rising water, fearful we would be swept downstream never to be heard of again. Eventually, the house was flooded, but that was shortly after we had moved away.

I found a job working as a bookkeeper at Prospect School, a progressive elementary school run by Bennington College. What did I know about bookkeeping? Nothing. However, I managed, loved the open classroom, the progressive teaching style, and Christopher was allowed to attend for free. Martha was still too young and went to daycare – that by the way had a monkey attending as well – great entertainment. We never gave a thought to possible disease or bites from this beloved animal. After a year at the job, I resigned and decided to try to earn an income as a potter. Fortunately, Christopher was allowed to stay on at the school through the fourth grade.

Ted was our landlord. His barbershop occupied one of the front rooms of our house. A locked door between Ted's shop and our living room opened only when we asked Ted to come in and kill wasps in our bedrooms. He was most obliging. Wim so appreciated Ted's attitude that he raised our low rent voluntarily. The house was old with a partial basement. There I set up my studio. We put a door from the street into the front room and turned it into a pottery shop. We lived in the kitchen, separated from the shop by a bead curtain. I rigged a doorbell by stringing a wire from the front door to a set of metal spoons in the kitchen. They would clang whenever customers entered.

The kitchen was large, accommodating a table, chairs, cupboards loaded with craft supplies and a large box holding scraps of wood gathered from building sites. The kids spent many a day sawing and nailing these together to construct all kinds of things. In addition to cooking, a lot of other projects were launched in that room: games, puzzles, crafts and artwork.

In those early days, we were beginning to wake up to the dangers of ingesting preservatives, vegetables grown with artificial fertilizers, hormones, antibiotic injected meats, and readymade foods. These products were good for keeping American corporations rich but not good for keeping American citizens healthy. Our budget was stringent, based on a teacher's salary and my part-time job. It was a challenge to pay for healthy food. We had a community garden across town but the harvest was limited.

No meat was served in our house for a number of environmental and health reasons. I tried to buy only organic fruits and vegetables. Most meals consisted of chickpeas or soybeans in various disguises: cookies, casseroles, burgers, soup, you name it. Not disguised enough apparently. The kids didn't exactly wolf down their food. I was hardly a gourmet chef and became easily distracted. The fire alarm was our dinner bell. On one occasion when Christopher asked if his playmate could stay for supper, his suspicious friend asked, "What are you having?" I told him and he said "Nah, I'm going home." After he left, I turned to the children and told them I didn't know what they did when invited to someone else's house for a meal, but they were *never, ever* to ask what was being served, that it was horribly rude and impolite to do so. I turned around and discovered, to my embarrassment, that the kid had never left. Maybe he learned something.

Friends felt sorry for the children. Perhaps they were right. In fact, my husband felt sorry for the kids too and, from time to time, would secretly take Christopher and Martha once a week to McDonald's. This was enormous fun for the children because they rarely went out for meals – not in the budget. None of them let on what they were up to until years later. At least I saved their future spouses from hearing "you sure can't cook like mom used to."

Despite our meager income, we got by pretty well. One year though, we were scared into selling our wedding silver, an oriental rug brought from Holland and our piano in order to pay our taxes. Raised to believe that those who didn't pay their debts deserved to be locked up, I had panicked. I was unaware there were provisions for paying taxes off slowly. That same year, a wealthy friend of my father boasted he had paid no taxes at all. That was a wakeup call for me. There was definitely something unfair about the financial laws in this country, even back then.

We lived in Bennington from 1969-1974. I worked my pottery fulltime and had an apprentice as well. The Civil Rights Act, passed in 1964, led us to hope for a future free of prejudice, one full of tolerance and decency. We marched in protests against the war in Vietnam, against segregation, the Kent State murders and environmental pollution. Christopher would ask, "Can I go to Little League today?" and I would answer,

"No, we're going to march." Poor kid.

We not only protested but held music jams at our house... with some of Wim's students playing guitar and burning their draft cards. Tea was offered at all hours, coffee sometimes when we could afford it. Friends came and went throughout the day. It was a time of breaking with convention, of belief that we could bring about a more peaceful, healthier culture. We cared about philosophy, not security. I began to realize I didn't need to own things to admire them – which was a good thing as we sure didn't own much.

The antiwar momentum was swelling in response to the government's constant reports that we were killing gooks not people and if we didn't stop them there, they would destroy America. Who would imagine that not forty years later, Vietnam would become a major tourist destination for Americans. So, again, what was the point?

As a potter, I made not only pots but peace pipes – smoke what they wanted – and an antiwar chess set, the board and figures in orange and black Halloween colors. The pieces brought the message: the pawns were children with lollipops and guns; the knights were hobby horses in the grip of giant hands; castles were machinegun turrets; bishops held crosses in front and grenades behind the back; queens were coiled snakes and the obese greedy kings had claws for hands. The set was bought by a man who designed an entire room around it.

I held séances at the house, studied the paranormal and brought psychics to town to give presentations. Exploring the realm of the spiritual was exciting. Did I ever see auras or get messages from the dead? Never. The only close encounter was experienced by the dog who started growling and pacing in circles around our candlelit séance.

When Martha was 6, she once spent an overnight with a bunch of kids who terrified themselves (but not Martha) by telling ghost stories. She calmed them down by explaining that ghosts were friendly. Familiar with my attempts to reach out to the "beyond," she considered the supernatural to be natural, not something to fear. Christopher, however, at the age of 5, showed early signs of skepticism. I had been driving him to kindergarten. He was sitting in the passenger seat beside me (era before seatbelts) when I warned he better be a good boy because Christmas was coming and Santa's elves were out watching.

"I don't believe in elves," he said. I told him that was rather foolish as I had just seen one run out of his boot (that was lying on the floor mat where he'd kicked it off). A minute later, glancing to the side, I saw him stretch out his leg and with his toe, tip the boot up and peek inside to check if there were more. The beginning of a questioning mind.

Did the '60s make a difference? Trying to bring about change was like kicking leaves. Things whirled up then most often, quickly settled right back down as they were before. Change takes time, often many years. We did stop the war in Vietnam and fight somewhat successfully for civil rights. However, we did not change the mainstream culture into a less greedy, kinder one, nor did we wipe out racism. What I have tried to do since is, in small ways, give meaning to that era by taking on the establishment whenever it tramples on the less fortunate.

With the best of intentions, we often went astray. The effect on Christopher of all this anti-war activity was not what we had hoped. He was bedeviled with nightmares. Only in later years did we learn he had been terribly afraid of being sent to fight in Vietnam. I had frightened him of war just as my father had frightened me of the Communists. Things go round.

We grew concerned about Christopher's self-image when he later started signing his school papers as Christ. We asked the teachers what they thought that was all about. They grinned and explained he was only signing Chris T. (for Tissot).

Meanwhile, Martha was creating her own special world. When she was old enough, we sent her to a nursery school run by Bennington College. One day I was called in to the office to talk about the trauma Martha had suffered. "What trauma would that be?" I asked nervously.

"About her sister falling off the roof and dying."

"First I ever heard of it," I replied. Martha's imagination developed early – she knew how to make up wonderful stories *and* how to get attention. The interning teachers, somewhat misled, had been proud of their hard work helping her cope with the death of her sibling. Eventually, everyone became used to Martha's storytelling. One morning, when I was walking her to kindergarten, a terrified deer dashed blindly onto the main street, nearly wiping her off her tricycle. It was a very close call. On arriving at school, she told about her adventure. That time she was roundly admonished by the teacher for making it up.

Another day, Martha was followed home by a classmate who ran into our kitchen, grabbed a picture of her grandparents in a frame she had made, ran outside and threw it in the river. Martha was in tears. I was irate. It was three in the afternoon. Dragging her along, I walked over to the housing project where the boy lived and told the mother what had happened. Suddenly there was a roar from the back room and the father came staggering to the door, dead drunk. "What did the little bastard do?" he stormed, "I'll kill the creep."

At that, I said "It's all right, he didn't do anything," took Martha by the hand and we beat a retreat, explaining to her how sad a life this child had, how jealous he was of Martha and how we should just be grateful for our own good fortune.

Bennington, except for the college bearing its name, was economically challenged. The neighborhood near us was so poor that Christopher's little friends (I use the term loosely as he used to have rock fights with them) took to stealing, not his toys but his *underwear*; a good lesson in how well off we were compared to others. Were we also poor? No. We did not have much by American standards. However, we had what mattered: food, shelter, curiosity, education, opportunity and Hope. In true poverty, those things are missing. We had neighbors with tremendous courage, neighbors who really were poverty-stricken, who struggled to heat their rentals and put food on the table. They were a source of inspiration for me: often generous, kind and cheerful regardless of leaky roofs, broken down cars and poor health.

Frequently our reaction to serious events was laughter. At one point Wim was fired from North Adams for refusing to wear a cap and gown at the graduation ceremony. He didn't feel the students' academic achievement deserved that kind of respect. He was fired in June. The students protested his firing. Even some of *them* thought they didn't really deserve those diplomas. He was hired back several weeks later. We just thought it very funny.

We had a friend, Eddy the Arab. Eddy disappeared for a year, then turned up deeply tanned. "Been in the islands?" we asked.

"Nope. Been in prison, working out in the yard."

It seems Eddy had been at a rest stop on the Mass Pike when he noticed a bus left running and filled with Smith College girls. The driver was making a pit stop. Eddy jumped on the bus and drove it away, the girls laughing and singing; the cops chasing them down the highway. "It was great fun," he declared, "well worth the year I paid for it."

CHAPTER 10

Career Change

Dreamers that we were, we had hoped to eventually each work part-time, leaving our days free for family and activities. We were not going to let the pursuit of money run our lives. But times were changing and one fulltime salary no longer supported a family as it had before. My pottery sales were up one month, down the next. It was not a dependable source of income. My bookkeeping job had left me unfulfilled. The local hospital offered a Licensed Practical Nurse program. I enrolled, partly for financial reasons, partly because I wanted to know how people coped with hard times, and if I could help make a difference to those who suffer.

I also had another reason for wanting to be a nurse. I had been fascinated by the world of medicine due to my own health problems. Robin and I, both serious childhood asthmatics, had had some close calls. When we were very young, there was little treatment available. You survived or you did not. Mother never let on that we were in any danger. Because of this, we children stayed calm even when struggling for every breath. Her instincts about health were excellent. She did not let asthma hold me back from doing whatever I wanted. I remember carrying a big contraption in my pocket that looked a bit like a perfume atomizer. It had a rubber ball connected to a glass bulb with a spout about three inches long. If I felt an attack coming on, I squeezed the ball and inhaled a couple of doses of medicine, mostly with questionable success.

But when I was an 18-year-old, I had my closest call with the grim reaper. One evening, used to asthma, I toughed it out way too long before telling my parents I needed to go to the hospital. There was a blizzard that night. Dad threw an anvil in the back of the car to give it extra weight and make it more maneuverable on the slippery roads. My parents and I headed for the emergency room 19 miles away. Twenty minutes later, we nosed into a snowdrift. It was the middle of nowhere. Dad set out walking, heading to the nearest farmhouse for help. We watched him disappear into the storm, fearful he would lose his way. If he was not back in an hour, he had told us, mother should also set out.

I sat straight up in the back seat, in severe chest pain and fighting for every raspy breath. It was cold, dark and quiet, except for my breathing. All I could think of was the Russian story about the wedding party on a night sleigh ride fleeing from wolves. Every once in a while they would throw a member of the party over the side to try to slow down the pursuit of those ravenous beasts. I asked Mother to tell me a story. "I can't think of one," she said, for the first time at a loss for words. In the past, Mother had sat by my bed many a night telling stories to help me through the long asthmatic hours. It turned out the Russian sleigh story was the only one she could think of as well. We waited an interminable hour without Dad reappearing. Mother was about to leave and set out herself when through the whirling snow we saw headlights. It was a snowplow. Following it was an ambulance which I refused to get into, barely able to move and terrified of being forced to lie down. That would have killed me. So instead, my dad got back in the car and we sped off to the hospital where it was discovered I had completely collapsed one lung and 90% of the other. Chest tubes were inserted, an oxygen tent set up, injections given and private nurses called in. That was in 1959 when there was no such thing as an ICU. I recovered in ten days but continued to have asthma all my life. I was impressed with the world of medical knowledge that had saved my life and had always wanted to learn more. Now, I could follow my earlier interest by enrolling in nursing school.

Meshing Children and Work

Mornings, I had to be at the hospital by 7 AM. Christopher, still at the Prospect School, took the bus a half-hour before I left. Free tuition was extended to our son at the private school because I had worked there, but they could not afford to extend that to Martha too so she attended first grade at the neighborhood public school. She left a half-hour after I did. I would lay out her snowsuit, mittens, hat and boots in proper order on the floor. Then I set an alarm clock to alert her when to put everything on and leave home. It worked beautifully. Back then, social services had not yet stuck its nose into proper childrearing – thankfully.

A year later when Christopher was in fifth grade, now also at the local public school, he came home and asked why the teachers warned all the kids to cross the street and avoid a certain house full of hippies. "That's where all our friends live Mom. Why don't they want me to speak to them?" Why indeed? I explained that society does not approve of those who look and live outside societal norms. Never overlook the strange ones – they may well become our culture's most creative and innovative leaders.

Days were not always calm. There were rough stretches as well. We had planned to take a few of Wim's students on a trip to Holland during summer break. They came to our house one evening to make plans for the excursion. Driving home afterward, they were hit head-on by a large

Cadillac roaring out from the nearby race track. Two of them were killed. It was devastating. I became acutely aware how life hangs by a thread that can so easily break. Cherish the day.

In addition, Wim's and my relationship was not always smooth: two independent personalities clashing. At times we separated, always reuniting shortly thereafter; he missed the kids, we missed each other. We brought essential balance to one another's lives and shared many common interests, the children being one. They were a joy.

Martha was petite, blond haired, full of mischief, cute – and adored her brother. She often wore lovely gingham dresses made by my mother but that didn't suppress the tomboy in her. She was up for anything: fort building, tree climbing, and gravestone climbing (the cemetery was our backyard). Christopher was skinny with long hair, good-looking, and energetic. He remained so thin that for three years he wore the same beloved leather pants custom made for him by a friend. Every once in a while we would patch the knees and sew another strip onto the bottom of the cuffs, but I don't remember ever washing them. I think they would have stood up by themselves from all the years of accumulated dirt.

Christopher was always busy: fishing, biking, building, making pottery, or exploring the neighboring woods, rivers, and cemetery. Martha, not to be outdone, tagged right along. We took them both skiing but could not afford to ski ourselves nor to give them lessons. That didn't slow the kids down a bit. They followed along the edge of group lessons, put the instructions to work and so became good skiers. They were fun, smart kids and the center of our lives. Concern for their well being carried us through the storms.

For Christmas each year, we roamed church fairs for used toys. We found wonderful ones and the children were happy. The greatest success was a big, battery operated doll. When I squeezed her hand, her eyes lit up like flashlights. Weird. Martha found her on Christmas morning and came dragging "big baby" up the steps to show us. The doll was close to half her size. Soon after that, she gave her a haircut and bath. The water came pouring out of the many air holes in the doll's chest and the blue beacon eyes never worked again – fortunately. Martha still adored her.

When Christopher learned there was no Santa Claus, he was ecstatic. "You mean you spent all that money on us? I thought we never had any. That's so cool." He couldn't believe how generous we had been (not sure what that said about us), nor could he wait to join in and play Santa for Martha.

I especially wanted the children to grow up nonjudgmental, with awareness and understanding of other folks' misfortunes. Coming from a critical family, it was something I struggled with myself. I did not want to pass that attitude on to them. But I also did not see how they could become more compassionate without first going through their own suffering; that, of course, we did not want either. It was a conundrum. Perhaps it was part of the reason we gave them a lot of freedom to make mistakes on the theory that guilty of one's own failures makes us less likely to point the finger at others.

Hovering parents we were not. But if they forgot to make their beds, I called them home from school to do so. If they did a sloppy job of chores, I required it be done over. If they complained the teacher was angry with them, I asked what they had done to make him or her that way. If they whined about boredom, I set them to work cleaning the house. Today, the children still remember my favorite slogan: "No Whining." Martha tells me she never knew what that meant; no wonder my admonition fell on deaf ears. I was harder on the children than Wim, but I was most often at home to oversee their youth. If they wanted a toy (except at Christmas and birthdays), we told them to work for it. Looking back, I think I was at times too tough but what was done, was done.

This tough love approach was inherited from my mother. She had grown up in a household of five girls and an older brother. Her father, the Chief Justice of the Supreme Court of Virginia, (who died when I was five) was a busy man and frequently absent. Her mother was an invalid, often bedridden and waited on by maids. This grandmother died before I was born so I never knew her except from stories.

I had the impression that my mother and her siblings pretty much raised themselves, along with some oversight from the raft of black servants living on the premises. It sounded a bit like *Lord of the Flies,* each child vying to outdo the others. The only recollections Mother had of her mother seemed to be when she was called to her bedside for punishment in response to neighbors who dutifully reported any misbehavior. I know at least one time that punishment consisted of being lashed on the legs with sticks, and another time when she was a 7-year-old, being sent away to her room at the start of her birthday party, denied both cake and games. The offense? She had dug up a dead cat and chased her guests with it. Nobody else was providing entertainment so she did the best she could. Her mother offered little guidance for the day when her daughter (my mother) would have her own children.

Mother did her best, loved us fiercely, had an eye for beauty and taught us much about nature, as did Dad. We took walks, studied birds, wildflowers and ferns, felt the wonder of the still pond waters in the early dawn and purple evening mists at the end of day. I had plenty of freedom, often wandering on my own to explore the surrounding woods and fields.

But Mother could also be hard-nosed and prejudiced. She found fault with all my childhood friends and had criticisms galore for those in her own social circle. As for pets, she let my white mouse die when I forgot to give him water: a lesson in responsibility. Even the dog did not escape. One particular puppy did not show much affection for her. Mother got mad and gave him away to a pet shop. A week later, the dog escaped, miraculously found his way across the city of Worcester to bark again at our house. I was overjoyed and let him inside whereupon he immediately grabbed me by my braid and lovingly dragged me over to his old basket. Mother was furious at being ignored in preference to me. "After all," she said, "I am the one who fed him." The dog paid dearly for that oversight and was given away for good.

Our daughter Martha, like me, was and still is a great lover of animals. I vowed never to apply such strict discipline to her or all the many creatures she kept. She took good care of them without my having to chastise her for negligence. In my youth, I had rehabilitated several beasties. My very first pet was a June bug, named Junie. I was 5 years old and put him in a terrarium, not realizing he could fly. He did. I searched for him without success. Heartbroken, I was going for a nap when I stepped on Junie and slid 3 feet on his innards. Big bug. First of many pet traumas.

Mother, to her credit, was tolerant of the creatures I kept, as long as they were cared for. At one time or another, I acquired an injured robin, a skunk, a mink, a raccoon, a red squirrel and other assorted four-legged and winged creatures. I remember a guest staying with us in our city house who wanted to take a bath but said there seemed to be a hamster living in the tub. Mother apologized profusely and directed him to the other bathroom. Shortly after that he came downstairs to report there was a blue jay living in *that* tub and he guessed he would just settle for a shower.

June the raccoon was one of my favorites. Dad built her a large climbing cage, but most of the time she ran free, searching for mussels on Brooks Pond's sandy bottom while I went swimming. June was also allowed to run loose in the house. Unfortunately, she was quite vicious toward anyone but me. One evening, I heard a loud cry of distress from Dad. Mother and I rushed onto the porch where we found him stretched out on the glider, June sitting on his chest with both her claws clasped around Dad's cocktail glass. Having removed the ice and thrown it on the ground, she was trying to dip her nose in for a drink. Every time Dad moved, June bared her teeth and snarled. "Get this damned beast off my chest!" he yelled. Mother and I helped by bursting into laughter.

Ever since living in Connecticut, biking had been a part of our family life, a holdover from our days in Holland. In Hartford, I had attached a child's seat on the back of my bike, riding Christopher every day through the city traffic to the rose garden and play-park. I remembered my own lonely youth and wanted him to meet plenty of other kids. In Bennington, it was again my only means of transportation as Wim needed our car for work. I did everything by bike, including shopping. With a week's worth of groceries hanging off the handlebars and luggage rack, I would shoulder a loaded backpack, tuck Martha into the youth seat and off we would wobble – on the constant edge of crashing. By this time, Christopher could ride his own bike. Helmets? Who heard of helmets? We lived dangerously and survived just fine. We rode to the swimming pool, to shops, to friends and to the community garden we cultivated across town.

While living in Bennington, we invited a couple with three young children to stay with us in our small house. They had been traveling the country in a VW bus, finally deciding to settle in our town. Winter was approaching. They needed a place to stay until affordable quarters could be found. The five of them slept on the floor in the front room, the pottery shop. Suddenly, we were a commune. It worked out pretty well until one child came down with staph. It spread to the rest like wildfire. Over a couple of weeks, one by one, we presented ourselves at the emergency room for treatment. Our residence became known as the house of horrors. It was pretty embarrassing, but even *we* began to think of it that way. It took a long time for everyone to recover. The family finally moved out into low-income housing. They were creative, interesting folks. We remained friends for many years.

Our habit of welcoming overnight guests to bed down on the floor was reflected in our daughter's dollhouse. During one of my conservative mother's visits, she asked why all of Martha's dolls were thrown on the dollhouse floor. Martha explained they were not *thrown* there, they were guests *sleeping* there. This clue to our family lifestyle did not sit well with grandma.

New Directions

After three years at North Adams State, it became clear that Wim could not secure a future in college teaching without a doctorate. Not having completed his studies, he had to leave. He went to work at a boys' preparatory school, Worcester Academy in Massachusetts, coming home on weekends when he could.

I stayed in Bennington to finish nursing school. A paper was required before graduating. My interest in alternative food choices led me to write about the importance to health of eating a farm fresh, meat free diet – a totally radical idea for the times. I based my paper on the book, *Diet for a Small Planet* by Frances Moore Lappé. I received a good deal of skepticism for my efforts. My parents were so horrified by our vegetarian diet that when we visited there, they made a point of serving us meat at least twice a day.

I graduated as an LPN in 1969 and did pretty well except in pediatrics, nearly failing that course despite being the only student who had children. Typical was my answer on one of the exams. When asked what a nurse should do if she walked into a little boy's hospital room and he was masturbating, I answered: nothing. The correct answer: give him a fire truck to play with. At least I came to understand why guys chase fire trucks around every time a siren goes off.

After graduating, I took a job in a purportedly excellent nursing home. This second experience with such institutions was as appalling as the first. The building was lovely, the care abysmal. The aides were excellent, but there were not enough, just as I'd experienced before. The RNs in charge sat at desks doing little; the aides ran like crazy trying to care for everyone. My LPN position put me in the middle. I passed out medications, nursed the patients and reported to the RNs. Nobody seemed to care about the short staffing. Finally, in a fury over such a bureaucratic attitude, I stormed into the director's office (not the last run-in I would have with the establishment). She had been one of my teachers in nursing school. "How dare you treat people like that?" I demanded. "It is inhuman. It is not how you taught us to care for others. We need more aides to care for patients. We need the RNs out on the floors working, not sitting behind desks. Why isn't the kitchen staff setting up food trays for the patients, rather than just plunking them down out of reach?"

To my astonishment, I wasn't fired, but it was more kicking leaves. All remained the same. It doesn't pay to grow old in this country, unless there are dollars in your pocket.

After a year at Worcester Academy, Wim returned to graduate school at the University of Massachusetts, Amherst as a teaching assistant (free tuition and a small salary). We rented a U-Haul and in 1974 prepared to move again. I worked until the day before we left. Friends stopped by all those last hours to say goodbye. As a result, I got little done and so, by 5 o'clock, too tired to pack more, gave away most of the contents of our kitchen. I did regret that later.

CHAPTER 11

Vicissitudes of Campus Life

Amherst was everything one could wish: a five-college rural region, with access to good libraries and schools, international neighbors and free bus transportation. We started out in student housing where Wim and I slept on a pullout in the living room and the children had the bedrooms. I worked as a nurse in a Greenfield hospital some 20 miles distant. The children and Wim walked to their schools and work.

The '70s were lively times. Typical events in those years included the actions of a crowd of naked men and women who streaked across the parking lot to hurdle over a chain link fence – without apparent injuries. We applauded their success.

This period marked the height of the Indian meditation, yoga and spirituality movement, which was to have a long lasting and positive effect on American culture. The Maharishi initially attracted attention with the introduction of transcendental meditation. Many gurus followed in his footsteps, some valid, some not. People everywhere, myself included, were adopting forms of Indian philosophy. One particularly young guru visited Amherst at the time. Admission to his gathering was a dollar and a flower. Hundreds of people wearing patchouli oil, beads and sandals, flocked to pay up and learn from his "wisdom." The florists did well. He made a pack of money. The audience was uplifted. Perfect. Everybody was happy!

We met many fun and talented neighbors, including Reiner and Inga Ruft from Germany with whom we have remained friends for many years. Reiner stimulated Wim's love for music with renderings of George Brassens' songs. Inga enlightened me about the different approach to nursing in Germany which, unlike here, was patient, – not liability centered.

Martha suddenly took to sleepwalking. The first we knew of it was the frigid winter night she went outside at 2 AM. The door was locked and she couldn't get in again. Fortunately I heard the doorknob turning. Thinking it was a burglar, Wim got up and demanded what was going on. "It's me, Daddy. Let me in." That was alarming. We had to bar the doors after that so she couldn't escape. However, she was a Houdini. It was several days later at 4 AM when a knock on the door awakened us again. We opened it to find a friend of ours who lived two blocks away; Martha was in his arms. She had managed to unlock the door, go outside and walk barefoot across the snowy campus. Fortunately she'd stopped to pick up his daughter to go to school with her. (not all knocking in the darkness portends evil.) Martha, night-dreaming, was also prone to making phone calls at all kinds of ungodly hours. We didn't sleep well those days, constantly alert for sounds of our midnight prowler.

We were good friends with a nearby professor's family. Martha and David, their youngest, spent hours together, speaking a make-believe language in an imaginary world that no one else could enter. Eleven-year-old Christopher, on the other hand, had moved on to the real world where he hung out with David's older brother, Nicky. They used to sneak on the free buses (children not allowed) and travel, unbeknownst to us, all over the countryside. Their adventures were numerous, so were their arguments. Both extremely competitive, they once got into a particularly loud clash while playing Monopoly. Christopher was irate at Nicky for hiding his money under the rug. He set up a howl of protest at such cheating. Nicky pulled out his money, apologized and the game continued. Then, twenty minutes later, Christopher pulled out money hidden under *his* edge of the rug and declared himself the winner. Both were clearly destined to succeed – in one capacity or another.

Many days I kept the kids home from school. Working weekends, I had only the weekdays to be with them. We would visit museums, libraries, zoos, plays and exhibits, go skiing in the winter, or boating in the summer. We had an old rowboat with a 5-horsepower motor that we kept on the Connecticut River. It was called the *Dodder* (Named after a character in *The Little Gray Men*). The school was surprised by how often the children were sick. The kids never let on, nor did they object – my version of homeschooling. They were none the worse for it, maybe even better.

After a year, we moved to a lovely duplex just a block from our previous apartment. Surrounded by state forest, it was graced with large lawns sweeping down to a river at the far end. There was also a basement where, to my joy, I could set up my studio again.

We were determined to raise our children with no TV – no movies either. But someone, mistaking our philosophy for poverty (we were pretty deep in both), took pity on us and donated a large hulk of a television. When ready to move to the new duplex, Wim, annoyed with all the screen time the kids had been putting in, dragged it out to the metal dumpster and heaved it in. The TV landed with the sound of a bomb going off. Kids came running from everywhere to salvage the monster – to no avail. It was shattered. The children were back to entertaining themselves. This and a more general annoyance with kids' antics earned

Wim his only nickname: GRAMPS, after a character in the Donald Duck cartoons.

Meanwhile, at the hospital, my first assignment was in the labor, delivery and newborn section. The staff was good, the learning experience excellent. While I enjoyed the work, my preference was for something more challenging. Eventually, I transferred to orthopedics and rehabilitation. That was eye-opening and demanding. There I got a firsthand look at the true hardship caused by accidents, strokes and disease. I saw how good health is as fickle as the wind. I came to appreciate the tremendous courage some display when faced with incredibly hard times. It was humbling.

Wim studied, worked as a teaching assistant and supplemented our income with cleaning jobs. Money was tight so we qualified for free government surplus food. Every month we received fantastic natural peanut butter in a half-gallon metal bucket. It was so good there was a demand for it on the black market. We could have sold it ten times over, but it was too delicious and nutritious to let go. We also received excellent oatmeal, but the rest left much to be desired and explained why it was surplus: cans of stringy chicken, bottles of corn syrup, corn oil and enormous blocks of gluey, yellow American cheese. However, it did help us to more plentiful meals.

The stress was tough on Wim. He finished all his doctoral courses but couldn't find the time or peace of mind to launch on a thesis. In addition, I began to realize how difficult immigration was for him. He observed life with refreshing and often humorous insight. Life was never dull in his presence, often bringing unexpected twists and turns. It was what I loved about him. But his eccentric personality was not well suited for the job world. He found the American culture, under its perpetual smiley face, tough and unforgiving. He lacked the lingo and connections for the business world, the competitiveness for high academic achievement. So, we moved again, this time to New Jersey, where he was hired to teach, once more, in an exclusive preparatory school.

CHAPTER 12

"Joys" of Suburbia

In 1976, with another couple helping, we packed two U-hauls, bid our lovely house goodbye and set out for suburban Ridgewood, NJ. There is freedom in city life, freedom in country life, but the strangling conformity of suburbia had always scared me. "Don't put me in the suburbs," I pleaded. Wim said I was prejudiced. True. I was, with good reason it turned out.

He had found a duplex on a lovely quiet street. Upon arrival, so as leave the driveway free for the owner Joyce who lived in the other half of the house, we pulled onto the lawn and released the children and dog (Did I mention we had a Labrador retriever?) who all tumbled out of the trucks, bursting with energy after the long confining trip. Big mistake. Like a crazed witch, Joy came tearing out her front door and welcomed us by screaming, "Get the trucks off the grass, lock up the dog, and control your children." It was quickly apparent that chemically induced grass is sacred in suburbia – sterile green overly thirsty lawns devoid of wildflowers, ferns or moss. Don't mess with them.

I went inside, sank onto the floor, put my head on my knees and said, "See? Suburbia – it's just like I told you."

"Do you want to go back right now?" Wim asked. I did, but it was too late. Ties had been cut with the past. Suburbia continued to be all I had feared: stuffy, racist, exclusive, narrow-minded and intolerant. We were clearly not up to par. Wim found the atmosphere at the preparatory school hyper and hostile. It was not for him. Instead, he took a job at Columbia University's Butler Library. Thus began twenty-five years of lengthy commutes in and out of New York City.

Disturbing Days – and Nights

I was fortunate to find work at an area hospital. Nursing brought me what I sought: learning how folks handle their fragile or not so fragile lives and the chance to be of some small service at the same time. I saw both extreme suffering and extreme courage.

An event which made a strong impression on me was that of two patients I attended. One was a wealthy woman who had busted her back while skiing in another state. She was brought by private ambulance to our hospital so she could be near home and children. Her husband hired a nanny and maid, keeping things afloat until she recovered.

"If injured, it doesn't matter how much money you have, we all suffer alike," she proclaimed. Wrong. I was also caring for a single mom in a full body cast who had been hit by a drunken driver. She lay helpless in the hospital while strangers cleared out the apartment she could no longer afford, packed up her possessions, put them in storage and placed her children in foster care: job, home and kids gone in one fell swoop. How could she find the peace of mind to heal with so much turmoil in her life? Money does matter.

I had another patient, a gruff Mafioso turned witness. His buddies – bit of a misnomer – tried to kill him but botched the job. He was recovering in the hospital with a 24-hour guard outside his door. On going to wake him each morning, I would crouch below the windowsills, snap the shades up and wait for the gunfire. For some reason he found my actions annoying, but I wasn't about to lose my life over this guy. Not long after discharge, he was finally gunned down and killed.

One of my elderly patients died in the night. Part of postmortem care involves putting dentures back in a person's mouth. Her elderly roommate slept through the whole thing. I woke her in the morning, told her the other lady had been transferred, got her up for breakfast, went to retrieve her dentures and – oh horrors – found I'd put them in the mouth of the deceased. I told the patient they were in the utility room getting a good cleaning, then called the supervisor and explained. "I'm not going down to the morgue to retrieve them," she told me, "you are." I did and cleaned them thoroughly but after that, advised my patients to keep their teeth safely in their mouths or, better yet, send them home.

Dad, having run a successful industrial bank, had told me that suggestions for improving the workplace would always be welcome. How wrong he was. More often, egos, jealousies and insecurity stand in the way of practical considerations, whether working for corporations or nonprofits. That never stopped me from kicking leaves, but it did bring a good deal of trouble the rest of my working days.

While nursing was rewarding, the administration was intolerable. I started my days on a large, sorely understaffed, orthopedic floor. Two other nurses and I got together and asked for a team meeting to see if we could implement a more efficient plan for filling patient needs. For this suggestion, we were roundly disciplined and forbidden to work together again. I was called into the director's office. "You are thinking like management. You are insubordinate. It is not okay. You should just do as you are told." From then on, the supervisor trailed me around the floor harassing me constantly. "You should be in Mary's room, her breakfast tray is still on the bed, and you should… etc." Finally, fed up, I turned to her and listed off the many things that needed doing at that very moment.

"There is no way," I said, "with this shortage of staffing that we can get to everyone. It should be obvious to you by now." No answer. Once more I escaped firing. I was good at my job and they knew it. However, I was switched to the 11 PM to 7 AM shift. There I was delighted to find efficient, skilled and collegial nurses. All were equally happy to escape the overinflated daytime administration.

For patients, nighttime can be long and lonely. I found it important to lend a listening ear to those who lay awake, their dark hours filled with fear. I believe listening, and sometimes just holding someone's hand, was often as effective as medication. Not only did it help my patients make it through the night, but it gave me the satisfaction of knowing I could make a difference. I worked that shift for several years.

One time, I had to undergo minor surgery. I figured I would not sleep well the night before so might as well work the 11-7 shift as usual. In the morning, after preparing my pre-op patients for surgery, I got a big kick out of shocking them by hopping on one of the gurneys and being wheeled to the operating room at the same time. Anything to have a little fun.

Eventually, I transferred to the emergency room (ER), as well as the Intensive and Coronary Care units. In these areas, nurses are on the front lines saving lives. In these units, there was no time for infighting or bureaucratic nonsense. Every action, every minute counted. Once patients were transferred to the medical floors for follow-up treatment, the nature of work changed. Nurses did their best, but legal issues, bureaucracy, micromanagement and short staffing drove the care. I was appalled at the hospital's focus on profit rather than patients' well being. If I had stayed on those floors, I would have done some kicking.

If you want to see the underbelly of a community, hang out in an ER. That underbelly belongs not only to the less privileged but the overly privileged as well. For all the pretensions of upper class suburbia, sorrow and hardship undermine many of its families. In the ER, tragedy reigns, alongside miraculous rescues. There were suicide attempts, some successful, some not, by both adults and children. We saw car accidents depriving children of mothers and fathers, and accidents wiping out the children. There were heart attacks, life-threatening asthma attacks, shootings, runaways hit by drunk drivers and accident victims left brain dead. Family problems were frequent: parents beating their children – and children beating their parents, as well as feuds leading to hysterical paralysis and heart attacks.

But things could also end well. Lives were often saved by the quick response of ambulance crews and emergency room personnel. Those were the happy tales. Rather than dwell on the drama taking place, and there was more than enough of that, I like to think back to the funny episodes – funny in a warped kind of way because most of the time it was quite stressful. Comic relief was welcome.

In one incident, I was setting up a suture kit for a doctor to repair a severely injured patient. Once he arrived and started to stitch up the wound, I began to feel faint. Did I mention that I fainted easily? – a difficult habit to deal with in a hospital. I turned to the nurse on the other side of the curtain in the next cubicle, told her to come quickly and switch places with me. She was putting pressure on a patient's head wound to stop the bleeding. He was lying on his back on the gurney, dead drunk and talking nonstop. I took over, sat on a stool behind him, pushed down on his wound while leaning way over with my own head lowered to prevent passing out. From this position I talked to him. "It sounds like your voice is coming from the floor," he said.

"Ah," I responded. "That's what happens when you get drunk. You don't even know where voices are coming from. In fact, that's how you got into the accident that brought you here." I continued to lecture him on correcting his ways and he confessed as to how things certainly did seem to be upside down.

Another time the police came around with a photo of a wanted criminal who was on the loose. "We think he's injured so if he shows up here, call us."

"You've got to be kidding," we said to one another. He was the scariest looking dude we had ever laid eyes on. "If he shows up here," we mumbled, "we're out the back door!"

Thankfully, he never did appear. However, later that night we had a quiet spell so we dressed up the intern to look like the criminal. We sent him around to the ambulance entrance and had him stagger in the door. What a sensation. It was great. The doctor nearly passed out from shock.

In the middle of one particular night, an intern came running in from the darkened hall shouting that he had just been attacked. We dashed back with him to discover a drunk had managed to climb up into the drop ceiling in the waiting room, crawl along until he fell through above the front hall of the hospital, landing on the intern who just happened to be passing by at that moment. The invader broke his arm as he careened off the intern and hit the floor. We tried to take the accident seriously but could not stop laughing.

It was reported that one evening, former president Richard Nixon had arrived at our emergency room with a grandchild needing stitches. It was very busy so the child had to wait in the back for a while. Nixon was invited to go sit with him until the doctor was free. As he walked past the trauma victims stretched out on gurneys and dripping blood, he raised his hand in the victory "V," his signature trademark. Some habits are hard to shake. The response was muted.

You would think that becoming the director of a large emergency room would be achievement enough for any man. However, for one it was not. What a surprise to have the police march in and cuff our director. It seems he had put out a contract on his ex-wife. He was running a stolen car ring as well. Some folks just never have enough. I later overheard one of the doctors commenting that he'd always wondered how his Ferrari could have been stolen right out of the hospital parking lot.

Being a morning person, I found sleep during the day difficult. I was always up in the afternoon to be awake when the kids got home from school. I tried to stay up until I left for work at 10:30 PM. It was important that both parents be there for them. Exhaustion ruled my days.

Reaching Beyond

While nursing satisfied my need to help others, I also needed something more creative in my life. So, I set up a basement pottery studio (the fourth one), joined a craft guild and sold my pottery at various shows. Both Christopher and Martha would accompany me to these events. Christopher made wooden items which he sold there. Martha took books and would spend the day reading under my display shelves.

Many days I would sleep on the sofa with the alarm set to wake me every couple of hours so I could turn up the kiln temperature. Twice a week, due to nightshift scheduling, I was up 24 hours a day. Did I say the pace was exhausting? The hours were brutal. I could never adjust. Despite it all, I was still determined to spend time with the family and have fun. In addition, I was trying to salvage my creative identity by keeping my craft going. I would fall asleep at the most ungodly moments such as: at stop lights; when washing dishes; talking on the phone; or when reading to the kids. One time, when out for dinner with friends, I dozed off, my face falling into my plate of ravioli. Totally embarrassing. The man across from me turned to Wim and declared, "I think I'm boring your wife."

The children attended public school. In Amherst they had enjoyed classes; in Ridgewood they did not. We should have paid more attention to the name of the town – for rigid it was. There was no allowance for deviating from the path of righteousness, and that path was simply an extension of the corporate mentality. Go for the gold and if anyone gets in your way, stomp on 'em. Power and image ruled. School was competitive and a step to rising up the ladder, not a place to enjoy learning.

I sought more contact with liberal thinkers, thought I would find it in the world of art and crafts. But, here too, the corporate mentality had crept in. It was not so much about free expression as about following the trend, self-promotion and rubbing shoulders with the famous. This kind of thinking pervaded the literary world as well. I was quite in admiration of my cousin Deric Washburn who had, for years, persisted in writing plays despite gaining little national recognition. When I told him this, he responded that he was worn down by the lack of success and ready to sell out to Hollywood. The result was *The Deer Hunter*, a tremendously popular movie. It was a major accomplishment, but to achieve it, I think he had to play up to the big boys. Was it his best work? Perhaps. I'm not sure.

CHAPTER 13

Rigid in Ridgewood

The children struggled in suburbia. Martha, with pigtails and overalls, was roundly mocked by fifth graders who had already graduated to nylons and lipstick. Christopher found more acceptance through joining a prankish, scholarly indifferent group of boys, as well as playing team sports. But for both children it was a struggle. Drugging and drinking were rampant. Christopher managed to participate in both. I fear I set a bad example. As a going away present from a friend in Massachusetts, I had received a shoebox full of pot. I overheard the kids boasting about it to friends. Alarm bells went off. Our neighbors did not take lightly to such activities, at least not openly. Even more concerning, our next door neighbor was an FBI agent. Afraid of being turned in, I dumped the contents of the box into the toilet and flushed. The toilet overflowed and washed pot everywhere: on the bathroom floor, out into the hall and down the stairs where it was distributed around the living room. It took days to clean it all up.

It was nearly impossible to work full time, take adequate care of children and keep up with my pottery. When I still worked the day shift, I got a frantic call from Martha who was alone at home. Her gerbils had given birth to several babies. She knew the father would eat them. She was in a meltdown. "Take a piece of cardboard," I told her, "and slide it vertically into the cage. Separate the daddy from the mommy and little ones." She did. However, she separated mommy from the babies instead of daddy. By the time I got home, he had consumed all but one.

Those were rocky years for us. Suburbia was not a good fit. Some of Christopher's privileged friends had entire floors of the family home all to themselves whereas Christopher had little privacy at all; we had to walk through his small bedroom to get to our own. The children's' friends were dressed in the latest fashions, while Christopher and Martha wore thrift shop specials. I was a great believer in secondhand clothing stores: they recycled clothing, provided us with only slightly used quality brands which we could not otherwise afford, and supported good causes. I guess it was asking too much to expect our kids to share this enthusiasm. It was a wealthy prestigious area, a tough climate for children from a rural college town. However, they adapted by finding jobs, giving them disposable income, self-confidence and some status. They also got a dose of the suburban lifestyle they would choose to avoid in the future.

We did have a kind family next door and Joy turned out to be better than she first appeared. But another neighbor was heard to say we had no right to live there as I, as well as Wim, had to work for a living. That put us in the category of riff-raff. Tolerance did not thrive in suburbia.

At age twelve, Martha started working in the hospital tearoom. From there, she moved on to a waitress job at an Italian restaurant. She did so well and earned so much money that she leased a horse – and a trainer – and competed in horse shows. Christopher worked for a landscaping business owned by his math teacher. His extra money went into buying top quality clothes and a TV, which we couldn't very well take away from him this time.

I was not a patient mother. I'd had little contact with children before having my own. I couldn't understand why, at times, they were so difficult. When the children were young, we used to read the Laura Ingalls Wilder books to them. I would complain that they didn't behave like those perfect little frontier girls who, when upset, would stomp their feet and remove their bonnets. Shouldn't that be good enough? When Christopher and Martha rebelled, it went well beyond that. Martha once ran upstairs to her room, locked the door, opened the window and yelled out to the neighborhood, "Stop beating me Mom!"

I could do nothing else but open the kitchen door and yell out "I'm downstairs, I'm not touching her at all!"

Christopher, on being reprimanded, would sometimes disappear for hours at a time, knowing that would worry me and I'd be relieved to see him when he showed his face again. Other times he chose to duke it out – verbally – with me. Martha, wise little sister, would sit next to him and whisper, "Chrissie, just don't say anything," knowing the storm would pass quicker if he stopped talking back. I thought as a mother I should have the last word. Christopher was unaware of that fact.

I also hadn't realized that children have only partial vision. They failed to see clothes on the floor, doors left open, dishes in the sink and junk on the stairs. They lacked full hearing as well. When I demanded they clean it all up, my words fell on deaf ears.

Teaching kids to think for themselves made childrearing considerably more difficult. When they criticized someone, I tried to explain the situation from that person's point of view. To teach them awareness, I encouraged analyzing the gimmicks advertisers use to make us buy their products. However, that lesson was only partially successful. They still wanted brand name clothes. But think for themselves they did.

We were adamant that the children should live the life we could offer and not beg their wealthier grandparents for fancy clothes. One winter's day, 10-year-old Martha returned from a solo visit she had made to them. She was sporting new clothes, a new winter coat and boots. She assured me she had never asked, but it turned out she had calculatingly left her snow boots at home and taken only a few old dresses. When grandma commented on her inadequate clothing, she just shrugged her shoulders and put on a sad face. It worked; she came home with a fancy wardrobe. What a creative child.

When the kids complained about unfair treatment, rather than rush to solve the problem, I would respond, "Life is unfair. Learn to deal with it." We rarely interfered, though once Wim talked to the principal about Martha being unmercifully ostracized by fancy-dressed classmates. It actually helped.

Christopher soon had a paper route. With his profits, he bought a nice bike that he repeatedly left unlocked in the front yard. Finally, to teach him a lesson, I hid it in the basement before going off to the town pool for a swim. He came home, discovered it gone and complained to my friend next door who drove him around searching the neighborhood for two hours, finally taking him to the police to report the theft. Tough love. Also rather embarrassing. Two years later, in an act of retribution, he hid my bike on me. I went through the same rigmarole, becoming extremely upset at the loss of my bike. Then he confessed. Tough love. It's never easy raising kids.

Wim went a step further. One time he took a 20-dollar bill out of his pocket, lit it on fire and burned it to ashes in front of both children. "Don't let money rule your life," he said. The irony was that our lack of interest in making money backfired. Our life was ruled by the absence of it, not by the excess. Both kids, wise little tykes, took careful note.

We lived at constant odds with our Ridgewood surroundings. Sometimes, after finishing work on the 11 PM to 7 AM shift, I invited my fellow nurses to our backyard for a glass of wine before everyone headed home to bed. The neighbors, unfamiliar with the need to work and especially that people actually had to work *all night*, howled about our immoral behavior. Other unacceptable decisions included making our kids walk the mile to school instead of driving them – totally neglectful parents. And for transportation, we were actually caught using bicycles instead of our one car that Wim had to take to the train station every day. While we tried to raise the kids to be color blind, those around us did not. They shunned other races. One neighbor told me she was sick of short Orientals with their smiley faces and nasal tones – non-whites not welcome in the neighborhood.

We had a Mexican friend and neighbor, a professor at Teacher's College, Columbia University, who declared he would show us how real Mexicans drank Tequila, the kind with a worm in the bottle. One evening, we sat in the backyard together, opened the bottle and imbibed – some more liberally than others. I had to go to work that night. When I left, Wim and his friend were both in a stupor, legs stretched out in front, chins on their chests. I heard later, that when our friend got up to leave, he walked right through his precious guitar. Fortunately it was dark and the neighbors failed to witness this mortifying event.

At times, it was exciting to live near New York City. We took the kids to see some of the world's finest museums, plays and musicals such as *The King and I*. My uncle Gordon, curator of the Asia House, took us to a few Broadway shows as well: *Mummenschanz, The Elephant Man* and *Dracula,* to name a few. Expeditions to the city were thrilling and sometimes quite adventurous.

One time, a friend of mine, visiting from rural Massachusetts, asked to visit the Statue of Liberty. I drove her, her two children and our kids, all under the age of ten, to the ticket booth for Liberty Island. The kids had been constantly complaining during the long hot drive to the city. "I'll let them out here so they won't have to walk. We'll take the car to the parking garage around the corner and return immediately," I announced. Unfortunately, I made a wrong turn and instead of driving into the parking garage, drove into the Brooklyn Battery Tunnel. My friend, convinced the children would be kidnapped if not murdered, was in a meltdown. I assured her that all would be well – to no avail. It took us thirty minutes to find our way back. When we finally returned, we were greeted by four unfazed and happy children. Christopher and Martha had explained that Mom got lost a lot but had, so far, always turned up again.

Another time I planned a business trip to a hospital on Long Island. Wim had to drive into the city that same day and said he would drop me at the subway and that it would bring me right to my destination. "Are you sure?" I asked, afraid of getting lost and unfamiliar with New York trains.

"Absolutely, it's a direct line."

Beware the word "absolutely." I walked to the subway stop, went down the stairs to the underground cavern that housed the token booth, stores and coffee shops, and stood in line to buy a token. Suddenly, the side of the booth exploded in flames and smoke poured into the air. Figures, I thought to myself. "Oh shit," said the two well dressed, high-heeled women ahead of me, "Let's get coffee and split!" Get coffee? They had to be kidding! I was halfway back up the stairs just as they entered the underground coffee shop. Needless to say, the explosion, whose cause I never did learn, closed down my subway line. I became completely lost trying to find an alternate route. After riding trains for a half-hour, I opted to go above ground and figure out where I was. On emerging, I entered a shop and asked how far it was to the hospital.

"First of all lady," the tall, well-built male clerk told me, "*Nobody*, I mean *nobody*, walks in this neighborhood alone, it's way too dangerous. And second, you are still 2 miles away." Need I add that I walked … and lived to tell the tale? Yes, the city is a crazy place.

But none of my adventures matched that which our son was to have. He had driven into the city and, swerving to miss hitting a limousine, rear ended another car. A big burly driver got out of the vehicle and came pounding back to see the damage. Christopher was shaking in his boots. The rear end of the man's car was completely battered in; our son's car incurred hardly any damage at all. The other driver checked over his crumpled vehicle for a moment or two, then looked up at Christopher and said, "I don't see any damage at all, do you? No need to call the police."

"Yes sir," said our extremely lucky teenager as he hopped in the car and drove off. We didn't hear this story until years later. I still wonder about that other car. Was it stolen, the driver running drugs, a wanted man or even, perhaps, was there a corpse in the trunk?

CHAPTER 14

Escape

In 1982 we saw Christopher off to Keene State College, New Hampshire. The car was packed to bursting, Wim at the wheel, when our son suddenly jumped out, came back to where I was standing on the sidewalk waving goodbye, looked me in the face and exclaimed in surprise, "Mom, you're crying." Milestones are called that for a reason; they're hard. I was raised to reign in my feelings. The children rarely saw me get overly emotional. I think in this way they were somewhat deprived.

The rent for our duplex was raised higher and higher until we could no longer afford it. We looked for new quarters, joining the endless tide of folks who, making only modest salaries, are forced to live farther and farther from their jobs. This inability to live where one works, creates waves of commuters who lose hours of time traveling; commuters who burn fuel, pollute the air and are plunged into transportation insanity. We became vividly aware that a society built on this model leads to further lack of community, loss of family-time and a home life compacted into weekends. Wim had met folks on the Port Jervis train line who actually spent more hours traveling each day than they did at their jobs.

What to do? In 1983, Wim took control of the situation, finding affordable housing in Orange County 75 miles north of New York City. Admittedly I cried when I first viewed our new location, the then rural village of Washingtonville, NY in the Hudson Valley. It was basically a one street town, and that street was lined with a fair share of dilapidated houses. Once we made the move though, I came to see the place with fresh eyes and quickly became attached. And, I was glad we were no longer "doing time" in New Jersey. However, when faced with another move, I thought, due to my chronic state of fatigue that I just didn't have the willpower to go on, to pack up and move again. Somehow, we did it. Again we rented trucks, got help from neighbors and hauled ourselves north to a rickety but charming modest sized one-story rental house surrounded by woods and fields. Wim sacrificed much of his free time making the lengthy trip to the city, but he had helped his family to the start of a healthier life.

One day, I was collecting mail from our mailbox which was on a sharp curve of the road. A man pulled his car over into the left lane and asked for directions. "I'll give them to you," I responded, "but first better move your car to the other side before someone smashes into you."

"I asked for directions, not for a mother!" he responded as he angrily speeded away. When I told Wim about it, he laughed, delighted by the man's accurate remark. How humbling.

Martha transferred to the local high school where she was amazed to find the students welcoming, friendly and noncompetitive. She was suddenly quite popular. It did me good to see this happen. Meanwhile, Christopher, having dropped out of college and found a job, was still living with us. With two teenagers at home, the phone rang continually, day and night. When I was at work one evening, around 11 PM, Wim became so exasperated he leaped up, grabbed a pair of scissors and cut the telephone cord. "Why didn't you just take it off the hook?" I later asked.

"Because this way they clearly get the point. I don't want that damn phone ringing all the time." After splicing the line back together, the kids were still on the phone constantly talking, but it never rang again. Friends who tried to reach us complained we were never home. It turned out Christopher had stuffed cotton around the ringer.

I continued to commute to the hospital, a 50-mile trip, but I could now reduce my hours to part time, due to our lower cost of living. Wim had to make an even longer commute but could often go by train and subway, a somewhat less stressful means of travel. We met new friends, got outside more, paddled the rivers, hiked a lot and were generally happier.

Our landlord was a small-time Mafioso in the Queens trash business who, on weekends, drove north to his apartment over the garage behind our house. He was often accompanied by his bodyguard, Nick, who wore a cowboy hat and wary face. The landlord was a swarthy unkempt individual who packed a low slung gun and beer belly held up by a belt with a large bronze buckle portraying a garbage truck. If stray dogs entered the property, he would shoot over their heads to scare them. It didn't work and he didn't know why. "They're hunting dogs," I explained to this city man's mystification.

He insisted on calling Martha by everything but her given name; mostly he called her Louise. She couldn't stand him, nor could we. On her sixteenth birthday, he showed up with a present: a ceramic replica of a triple-decker McDonald's burger with all the trimmings: lettuce, tomatoes, mayonnaise, ketchup and cheese oozing down the sides. It was a music box that, when wound up, played the theme from the *Godfather.* The granddaddy of all kitsch.

This man prided himself on his superior culture. He told us how he once wanted to take his wife on a cruise with only the very best kind of people, so had booked their passage on the *Love Boat*. During the cruise, they had made friends with a highly educated couple. Next year, he said, they were all going to Australia and cruise down the Nile. I laughed out loud under the mistaken impression he was joking.

I made many good friends in our new location. One of them was John the taxi man, who in some ways was ahead of his time. He lived in a house built completely from recycled materials he'd picked up on the streets of New York. He brought them all north and constructed a house based on whatever he had found. It was a crazy construction, a bit like its owner, with additions jutting out at strange angles, tilted floors, and a hidden room accessed by climbing on the kitchen counter and opening a cupboard door. John was dirt poor but no dummy. He had managed to acquire land and build himself a castle.

I first met him one morning when, our car in the shop, John was to pick Wim up and take him to the train. He called at 5:30 AM to say he couldn't get the old girl started but was working on it. We assumed he was referencing his taxi, not his wife. Eventually, he showed up in a rust bucket of a van. Wim hopped in and made it to the train station on time. That night when John picked him up again, Wim had to run behind the taxi and push it until it started, then jump on board while it was rolling downhill. Quite a change from life in suburbia.

John was gaunt and dark haired with an oily pock-marked face. Due to his appearance and because of a history of mental illness, he was generally shunned by much of the community. Sometimes, when going to pick up a rider, the customer, shocked at the sight of the van and driver, refused to get in. That hurt. This was the same kind man who got up early five mornings a week to drive poor folks to their jobs whether they could pay or not. He particularly loved animals. When, on occasion, I used his service, he always put my dog in the front seat next to him, relegating me to the back.

He could never understand why someone would prefer walking to riding. If I was out strolling and saw him coming, I would hide behind a tree so he wouldn't stop and insist on giving me a ride. One time, on a cold December night, I was meeting Wim at the train station when we saw John standing on the platform, having just returned from seeing a doctor in the city. "Need a ride John?" we called.

"But I'm the taxi man. I'm supposed to give you a ride," he responded, as he got in the car and we drove him home. A few days later, just before Christmas, he showed up at our door to give us one of the most heartfelt gifts we have ever received, a precious box of eggs. He still couldn't get over the fact that we had actually given the taxi man a ride.

John took to visiting my studio, regaling me with stories about the locals that would have shocked them to hear. He was one of the kindest men you could ever meet ... except to his wife. He confided to me that she was becoming a real nag, mad all the time. "How so?" I asked. He explained that she objected to their Sunday rides because he put his girlfriend in the front seat, his wife in the back. "No wonder she's mad," I said, "Why do you do that?"

"Because my wife is boring; my girlfriend is not."

Big Jump

Shortly after we moved to Washingtonville, Marty Waterson, a wholesale representative, approached me with the intent of selling my pottery nationwide. I jumped at the opportunity as it meant not only that it would open up my market, but that I could attend fewer retail shows.

This was during the heyday of retail craft fairs. Participating in those shows required an enormous outlay of money and time. I didn't just send in an application, I went through an elaborate jury system requiring professional slides of my work, new lines every year and a long resume citing all the stores and museums that carried my pieces (Commercialism tainting the craft world; judging became increasingly based more on one's fame than on the quality of the pottery).

Then, for the show itself, in addition to first building up inventory, I spent a whole day packing my van, not only with all my pots but with a beautiful collapsible display my dad had made, multiple shelf components and a 10- by 10-foot tent canopy for outdoor shows. I often took camping gear and food as well. I did this about fifteen times a year, often getting up at 4:30 AM to make the 2 or 3 hour drive. Sometimes, if it was a one-day show, Wim or Martha accompanied me. It took three hours to set up the booth, six hours on my feet selling, then one-and-a-half hours to break it down before driving back home again.

If the show lasted two days or more, I made the trip alone, found camping nearby, set up my tent and, in the evenings, delighted in retreating to the quiet of the woods, a fire, a simple meal under the stars and a peaceful night. The day after the show, I was back at work again. Profits ran anywhere from $500 to over $2,000 a show, but it was exhausting. I hoped wholesale would provide me an opportunity to reduce the number of retail shows and maybe even give up nursing.

I loved making pottery, the way clay came alive under my hands as I spun the wheel, how it grew and changed as I worked, its wet, glistening sheen when just finished, the way it morphed into dry brittle clay, and finally, after a last kiln firing, into a durable, decorated pot.

I had often considered leaving nursing to make the entrepreneurial plunge into this work. However, it was a fairly risky move. I was burnt out on the frequent tragedies I witnessed at the hospital and tired of working on holidays. In addition, corporate thinking had come to dominate the healthcare field: it was all about profit, image and legalities. Last on the list were the patients. Then a friend told me that Wim had mentioned he might resign from his job and look for another. That did it. I figured if he quit first I would be stuck at the hospital for years. The very next day I went to work and put in my notice. My poor husband was broadsided. Not my finest moment, but I was now launched in a new full-time career. It turned out to be a success.

FAVORITE PLACES WHERE I HAVE LIVED, WORKED AND PLAYED

The Barn at Brooks Pond, our winter weekend home during my youth - 1959

*Standing by the Arno River, Ponte Vecchio in the background,
Florence, Italy – 1962*

*View to the far side of the canal from our Amsterdam apartment
on the Nieuwe Prinsengracht (canal) - 1962*

*Wim getting ready to skate (with me) across the Zuiderzee to the island
of Urk and back (30 miles round trip). Note the wooden skates.
Our first home, De Drommedaris, in the background - 1963*

Our delightful old fisherman's cottage on the Amstel River - 1963

*Christopher on a snurfer (forerunner of snowboards) in front of the
Cabin at Brooks Pond, Spencer, MA - 1969*

*Martha and her friend Teresa in front of the Pottery Shop,
Bennington, VT - 1971*

The Barn, Blooming Grove, NY. Location of my pottery studio - 1986

*Trailer life next to the pond. Wim getting ready for a bike ride, Rock Tavern,
NY - 1988*

Selling my pottery at the Kutztown Folk Festival, PA - 1990

Exploring the ghostly ruins of the castle on Bannerman's Island in the Hudson River. Nostalgic reminder of De Drommedaris - 1992

A stormy day on Long Island Sound. I join a kayak rescue team readying to paddle escort for a swim marathon. Wild day on the water! CA - 1995

Our snow-buried double-wide, Rock Tavern, NY - 1999

All volunteer built Ice Palace, Saranac Lake, NY - 2008

Trying my hand (and foot) at ice climbing - 2009

Our "Kit House" in the Adirondacks

The Village of Saranac Lake, NY - 2009

Taking a break out West on a hike in The Rocky Mountains - 2010

Loading up a snow-coach, ready to take us into Yellowstone National Park for a family ski trip - 2012

Family bike trip in The Netherlands - 2016

Revisiting (with family) the restored Drommedaris over 50 years after first meeting there - 2016

View from the cliffs on Baker Mountain of nearby woods and lakes. Saranac Lake, NY - 2016

CHAPTER 15

Challenges of Barn Life

In Washingtonville, our rental house had a basement where I continued to work. After a year the space became too small for my growing wholesale business. Jeanne and Felix, a generous couple living in the area, invited me to move my entire production into a large unheated space in the middle of their 18th century barn. Jeanne had a keen wit, abiding interest in the community and impressive knowledge of local history. She ran a charming gift shop at one end of the barn, a large post and beam space, heated by a wood stove, and packed with country gifts. Her husband, Felix, had a heart of gold coupled with a dry sense of humor that snuck up on the unsuspecting. He was a highly skilled woodworker. He occupied the other end of the immense building.

The 200-foot long barn was painted a classic dark red with white-trimmed, small paned windows flung across the front. Its black metal roof sported several shiny steel exhaust turrets along the ridgepole. It was as picturesque as a Currier and Ives, romantic and peaceful to contemplate. Inside, however, was a hub of activity. The barn snuggled into a hill: the first floor was on the ground level in the front, the second entered at ground level up the hill in the back. In addition to the gift shop, the barn was filled to overflowing with: Felix's woodworking machinery, lumber, piles of paperwork, boxes, spray booths, racks, work tables, saw horses, sawdust, a multitude of animals and constant visitors. It smelled of sawdust, paint, dust, dander and a much used coffee pot.

My windowless studio was tucked deep into the very center of this building where cows once stood in their stanchions. I kept their names tacked up on the wall: Bessie, Matilda, Flossie, reminders of the first occupants of my space. There was no running water. Each day, winter and summer, I had to tramp up the hill, prime an outdoor hand pump and fill buckets to carry back to the barn. In the winter, the heat in my studio came from firing up a couple of kerosene stoves. After an hour, the temperature would finally approach fifty and I could no longer see my breath; a tough work environment. I heated water on the stove, dressed in layers of clothes and drank numerous cups of coffee. However, the space was enormous, the price right, and Jeanne and Felix delightful. Furthermore, I no longer had to tramp through deep snow to reach my 6-

foot high gas kiln. There was a rock walled, dirt-floored room just perfect for it.

My studio was lined with shelves. There was a tiny office space partitioned off behind a plastic garbage bag wall, my version of construction. A 3-foot crawl space under one of the shelves was devoted to a mattress-covered pallet where our faithful dog Polo and his good buddy Brownie dreamed away the cold winter days, plunked in a heap on top of one another close to the stove. I had a couple of artists working part-time for me. When they were not present, I tuned to Public Radio, holding conversations with the dogs about the state of the world. They were a well-educated pair.

The barn's second floor was a storage area for everybody within a 30-mile radius. It contained a jumble of stuff: furniture, boats, old cars, trunks, crates, piles of slate, roofing tiles, lumber, even a stained glass Tiffany window as well as various building materials. I don't think anyone *really* knew what was there. Years of gray dust covered the lot, hiding a myriad of treasures. Sometimes, for entertainment, we would explore these "artifacts," discovering what had once mattered to others but not why. Like a museum, it revealed much about people who had lived and worked nearby. I unearthed an old iron three-legged pot with a long triangular handle stuffed down under an ancient pile of lumber in one of the outbuildings. No one laid claim to it, so the pot came to live with us where it now sits on our hearth and holds kindling and a load of memories. In a colonial museum, I found a similar one that dated back to the Revolution.

Though tucked deep in the barn's interior, I did not lack for visitors. They came, drank coffee, discussed food, environmental policy, art, music, local history, and anything else on their minds – a lively atmosphere. I even had one frequent visitor, an older journalist, who insisted he was a missing son of the Russian Czar.

At the time, I was particularly interested in foraging for wild, native food. Wim and I ate mushrooms, cattails, dandelions and all kinds of native greens and roots. Sometimes, on arriving in the morning, I would find a giant puffball waiting on my desk, or an unusual flower or some other odd item retrieved from the fields and woods. The barn crew knew I liked to try new things and often told me where to find interesting specimens. But when I invited them for a meal at our house, they would insist I serve take-out. They didn't trust my cooking and the thought of eating braised milkweed buds, wild mushrooms or pine tea set these rugged people a-trembling.

Working in the vast building, in addition to my employees and myself, were Jeanne and her helper Betty who manned the gift shop, Felix, three of his carpenters and a contractor and crew leasing equipment and space from him. Felix also never lacked for visitors. In fact, if you wanted to know what was going on in the area, this barn was the place to go. Bringing my eclectic friends into the scene made for a downright bizarre mix.

"A skinny guy in thick glasses and a black cloak just ran through our shop. Where did he fly in from? Another one of your friends no doubt!" the barn crew would mutter or "We rated all the applicants who came through here looking for a job with you. Sarah is a 4 but Natalie a 10. Hire Natalie." You can't change a culture overnight. I warned new employees about the sexist remarks. You had to be able to take it and give as good back. They always did.

One day, one of the guys came running into my studio yelling, "Come quick! A piece of wood just shot through George's ass!" Among the benefits of leaving nursing was not having to deal with terrible accidents. But there was no escaping this one. With a shudder, I jumped up and demanded my brand new employee, Monique, follow me to the scene. George, employee of a leasing contractor, had been working in a small room running trim through a molding machine. It had jumped off and shot through George's buttocks, stitching them together. He was standing inside a narrow doorway, facing out but unable to go further because he had 3 feet of 2-inch wide trim extending out either side of his butt. His face was ashen and clammy, his eyes dazed. Monique and I got on either side. We each held him up with one hand and steadied the trim with the other so that Felix could saw off the ends. We were dripping sweat and stress. I became even more nervous when Felix began to run the saw. My legs were frighteningly close to the blade. However, he successfully sliced through the trim and not me, the ambulance arrived and poor George was hauled away. In the emergency room, the doctors, fascinated by this bizarre accident, first took photos and only then removed the trim. As it turned out, no essential innards were pierced. The lucky dude.

Monique confessed later that she had been warned to expect the unexpected when she took a job with me, but this exceeded her imagination, nearly causing her to quit that very first day. Fortunately, she did stay on despite surprises that continued to interrupt our days.

It was several months before George dared to return to the barn, believing it had bad karma. He finally came back, failed to see an open trap door and dropped 9 feet onto a cement floor. We covered him up with a furniture blanket and called the ambulance again. It took so long to arrive that when it finally did, the guys had pulled the blanket over George's head and told the crew they were too late, it was all over (guy kind of humor). The crew heard George spluttering and whipped the blanket off. In the process they shook out years worth of sawdust throwing the patient into a paroxysm of coughing, further exacerbating his aching back. George turned out to be okay but never again returned to the barn.

Typically, the drivers of the big lumber delivery trucks were burly tough men. So one day when Felix received a call from Natasha asking him for directions to the barn, he couldn't wait to tell his guys. "A girl," they howled, "Wow! Can't wait to see what kind of chick this will be!"

Natasha arrived driving a big heavy duty truck loaded high with lumber. She backed that truck in just as pretty as we'd ever seen and emerged from the cab: a slim, leggy good-looking blond. "Guess we're going to have to unload this truck ourselves," said Felix. Wrong. Before they were even ready, she had climbed on top of the wood and started throwing it down so fast it took two guys to keep up with her.

"Way to go Natasha!" I shouted.

While a big wood stove heated Felix's shop, by noon my kerosene heaters had warmed my studio so that it was a lot more comfortable than the rest of the barn. Everybody squeezed into my small space to eat lunch, visitors and workers alike. We brought food from home or picked it up from the deli at the bottom of the hill. If we were short on utensils, one of the guys would make a fork or spoon from a scrap of wood turned on the lathe. For dishes, we took finished bowls from my pottery orders. After lunch, we let the dogs lick everything clean before placing the bowls on the shelves where they were to be washed before shipping. One of our visitors, seeing us place the saliva caked wares back in the orders, recoiled in horror. "You mean you just ship the bowls like that? Don't wash them?"

"Sure," we replied, "Don't you know you should always clean anything you buy before using it? This is why!"

Practical jokes were an on-going diversion; everything from tying a dead bat to my light cord (startling me when I reached for it in the dark) to Felix and Jeanne's kids throwing a snake at me that slithered down the back of my shirt and caused an explosion of language even the carpenters had never heard before. The snake turned out to be fake, but who knew?

Tamara, one of the artists I employed, was married to a man who worked for New York's sanitation department. Through him I became acutely aware of what a ridiculous throw-away society we have created. We could ask him for anything and he could find it on the streets of the city. If it was a microwave, he asked what size and brand; if a coffee table, how big and what material. In a little more than two weeks he would produce whatever we wanted. In fact, Tamara's house was furnished entirely with finds that she restored for her lovely eclectically decorated home. An inspiring example of what can be done by recycling. He even brought us eleven of Jacqueline Onassis's wine glasses, engraved with her initials, thrown out I suspect because they were not an even dozen.

In those days, we owned two old cars: one for Wim's commute, one for me. But as I didn't have far to travel, I got the one with no heat. When Wim's car was being repaired, he was forced to borrow mine. One the day the temperature dropped below 0. Wim took my car to the city and returned that evening wrapped from head to foot in a green sleeping bag. He looked like a giant caterpillar at the wheel. "You're crazy," I said, "what a dangerous way to drive!"

"I don't give a damn!!" he replied. "It was this or death by freezing!" That one time he showed good instincts for self-preservation.

The barn was a fire waiting to happen. It worried us all. In fact, I kept all my glaze formulas at home so I wouldn't lose those if it did go up in smoke. One night in January, 10^0 degrees outside with a fierce wind blowing, I got a call from Jeanne. "The barn is on fire," she said with resignation. I hopped in the car, slowly drove the 8 miles to my studio, not really wanting to arrive and witness the end of an era. All the time I kept thinking: Wim always asked me to bring the good pottery home instead of all the seconds. Now we have nothing left.

By good fortune, the volunteer fire department, just returning from another call when the alarm went out, managed to get there in time to keep the flames from spreading, though it had already consumed an addition, including the wood stove – source of the outburst. When I arrived, there were dozens of cars, trucks and residents from nearby towns filling the yard. The barn, however, to my enormous relief, towered above them, lit up by all the vehicle lights. I was hugely relieved, not only that it had survived but that the fire had not been started by my kiln that was powered by a 12-foot flame licking around the kiln interior before shooting up the chimney.

Though the firemen had stopped the flames from spreading, they were still concerned it might re-erupt. I went inside to find them in a tight knot over by the wall. On approaching, I discovered they were huddled around a pin-up calendar. "Hey," I shouted, "the fire is over here, not over there!" Red-faced and embarrassed, they abandoned their gawking and got back to matters at hand. By midnight, satisfied the blaze had been put down, we were faced with a new problem. To avoid a surplus of roast chicken, Brewster the rooster and his extensive harem had been sprung from their cages located inside the addition. With howling winds and frigid temperatures, we now scurried to capture these hose-soaked birds and get them into a warm area. The only place for that was the small room where I had turned off my gas kiln six hours earlier, leaving the room well-heated. Two sides of this room were lined with shelves of finished pottery. It was into this space we dumped the barn fowl, and it was here they dried out and continued to thrive for the next few weeks. How delightful to be greeted every morning by the cock-a-doodle-doo of Brewster, as he stood on the top of the kiln and greeted the rising sun. His wives had a harder go of it. Deprived of their nesting boxes, they adapted to their new surroundings by snuggling down on top of the 8-inch tall wine coolers where they laid eggs that promptly dropped the distance and smashed on the bottom. Lots of omelets. From that day on, instead of selling all my best pieces, I started bringing some home for us to enjoy.

The Rule of Animals and a Rock

And then there were the animals. Felix being a great lover of all that flew, hopped, slinked or trotted, kept a menagerie of creatures, both inside and outside the barn. At various times, the interior contained free-range rabbits, chickens, roosters, rats, dogs, cats, and of course, mice. It also contained Polo, the intelligent Border collie who ran my life. I hiked with him every morning before going to work and walked with him again later in the afternoon. During the day, he had free run of the barn and surrounding fields.

On a sunny afternoon, a stranger pulled into the parking area in a snazzy BMW with initials on the door. He entered the gift shop, leaving his well-groomed poodle in charge of the car. The vehicle windows were open. In a yapping high pitch, the dog demanded attention. Polo and the barn dog gave it to him in full force. Outraged by the intrusion of this city dweller, they attacked. With claws extended they leapt up and down against the silver initialed car. Oh horrors. We could not possibly afford the cost of repainting this man's vehicle. I walked quickly outside, as if I was also a visitor, threw the dogs in my car and drove away, not returning until well after the stranger had left. Honorable? No, but it staved off another financial crisis.

Felix had several dogs. When Clancy, a small brown one, went into heat, she was locked up in the barn to isolate her from roaming, crazed studs. Her only companion was our dog, Polo, who had been neutered years earlier. Later, safely past the danger point, Clancy was allowed her freedom again. Some weeks later, coming to work, I was greeted by "Hi Grandma."

"What's that for?" I asked.

"Just take a look at that litter of puppies. You'll see." There in a box, nuzzling Clancy, their brown long-haired mother, were six adorable black

98

and white puppies, each the spitting image of Polo. We never did figure it out.

So many animals lived in such close proximity that an identity problem developed. Clancy hung out with the cats. Fancying she was one herself, she often climbed onto the hoods of parked cars, then leapt-feline like to the roofs where she curled up for naps.

The chicken feed attracted not only barn fowl but rats as well. One rat grew so large on this easy source of food that the boss cat didn't recognize him for what he was. The cat would feed from the same dish right alongside the rat, assuming no doubt, that he was just another member of the family.

Many nights the rats romped joyfully across my wet pots, leaving tracks, poop and crumbled clay edges in their path. My employees were nervous about these critters, but I assured them there was nothing to fear; the rats had no interest in bothering us. Shortly thereafter, I was sitting at my desk eating my lunch when a rat jumped from behind my books and landed with a splash in my soup. Like a prissy city-girl, I screamed and leapt onto my chair to the delight of my crew. The rat population got so bad Felix reluctantly resorted to poison so we wouldn't be overrun.

In spite of several barn cats, the mouse population got excessive at times. Frequently, interior decorators visited the gift shop, the wood shop, and on a bad day, made it all the way back to my studio. They often wasted our time regaling us with stories of all the estates they had decorated and famous people they had worked for. One woman, dressed in stylish silks, lace and various fashion accessories, took a stand in the midst of my dusty chaotic workspace and let us know how important she was. While she talked, mice ran in and out under the hugely elevated instep of her high-heel shoes. I think they were playing *London Bridge is Falling Down*. It was hard to keep a straight face. Finally realizing what was happening, she made a wonderfully fast exit.

Another time, tourists had wandered around the barn and discovered an open back door leading to my studio. I had come in on Saturday to catch up on work. I was not particularly pleased to have three strangers invade my space and gape at me, a live working potter – as if they had dug me up on an archeological expedition. After hanging around and slowing down my production, one of them suddenly pointed in horror, struck speechless by what she saw. It was a bat slowly working his way up the length of a yardstick leaning in the corner. "Wha-wha-what is that?" she choked out!

"That's a bat, Uncle George I call him." And that took care of those visitors; they were gone in a heartbeat.

On one occasion, I had spent several days trying to phone a high-placed official in Washington to lobby for saving a beautiful piece of land in Orange County. Just as I finally got a connection, the rooster let loose right by my desk with a particularly rousing solo. He not only drowned out my voice but undermined my professional credibility. The contact was not successful.

Often, on morning hikes with the dog, I would carry back various items I had found in the woods: mosses, plants and oddly twisted twigs. One day I dragged back a large dome-shaped rock that was split horizontally halfway through, the crevice full of quartz crystals lined up like teeth in a monster's mouth. I left my prize on the guys' workbench to see what they thought of it. Their response was a delightful surprise. Returning later, I found those burly tough men huddled over my find. One imagined he was camping out on top of the miniature mountain; another projected a scenario in which a helicopter would fly over the top and lower supplies to the group stranded on the summit; a third speculated on what fun it would be to rappel down into the crevice and explore crystal formations. "But your ropes would get tangled," said another.

"Then, I would move over to the other side and drop down through this wider crack over here," he replied. They were completely engrossed in their fantasy adventure, high on nothing more than imagination. The effort I made to carry that rock to the barn was more than adequately rewarded.

CHAPTER 16

To the Barricades

When we moved to Orange County, NY from suburban New Jersey, I rediscovered my roots. Though I had grown up spending most of my time outdoors, in the years since then, I had become distant from the natural world. Now, once more, I roamed the woods and hills, absorbed nature's peace and let the healing earth rock me in her arms. Calm flowed back into my life.

In 1972, I was awed by the famous photo (sent back to earth by the crew of Apollo 17) of our lovely blue planet floating in space, encircled by wispy white clouds. Looking at that picture, I realized how small and vulnerable our tiny world really was. I kept that photo on the wall for many years: a reminder that we must all survive together, both man and beast, or all perish together. This sentiment was beautifully expressed in a famous quote written in 1972 by screen writer Ted Perry in a film called *Home.*[8]

> *"What is man without the beasts? If all the beasts were gone, man would die from a great loneliness of the spirit. For whatever happens to the beasts, soon happens to man. All things are connected."*

We grow an over-producing economy at the expense of the limited natural resources of an already exhausted planet. I found a perfect metaphor for this lack of logic in the historic house that Jeanne and Felix bought. It had no front door because, similar to the way we burn up our vital natural resources to gain greater luxury, the previous tenants had burned up their front door to gain a few more hours of heat. Brilliant.

Aware of man's murderous approach to wildness, I became active in environmental organizations. Having my own business and thus being more available, I was often the spokesperson for radio, TV and newspaper interviews. Reporters could always find me at my studio, face and clothes spattered with clay and, like a child, a key hanging around my neck (to prevent locking myself out of my car after hiking every

---

[8] This statement has been mistakenly attributed to Chief Seattle because in the film *Home*, it was written as part of his dialogue. Ref. Fact Check: Snopes.com

morning – something that had happened one time too often). On occasion, a reporter would return to interview me about my work as an artist. That was a nice side benefit.

The first time I added my voice to those rallying for land preservation was at an airport business meeting. Plans were afoot to cover 7,000 acres of beautiful open space, the airport's buffer zone, with roads and industrial warehousing. When I stood up to speak, official looking men shot contemptuous looks in my direction. Under their withering stares, my legs started to give way. Sheer panic. Get mad, I thought, not scared; they are nothing more than stiff pompous suits. That gave me the courage needed to stand tall and say my piece. That was my start in public speaking.

Many were the media adventures I experienced in those years. At one interview, a reporter let slip that Governor Mario Cuomo was visiting Stewart Airport to praise the "wisdom" of turning the buffer zone over to business cronies for development. Generally speaking, I liked Cuomo, but in this matter I believed he acted in bad faith. Only two of us were free to attend the address. On arrival, our presence was quickly made known and in no time we had a string of reporters following us around. "Watch her," I heard one reporter tell his cameraman, "She's up to something." Ah, the power of the press! With this kind of expectation, how could I disappoint them?

Soon the band struck up a tune, indicating that Cuomo's plane had landed, and he was about to enter the terminal. However, exactly which door he would enter, no one would say. The crowd blocked our view. The only empty space from which to see what was happening was atop the baggage conveyor belt (not running at the time). Perfect! I climbed up on it and was able to spot Cuomo and his entourage entering the far side of the terminal. I reached the governor easily by running along the belt, reporters in tow down below. When I arrived right in front of him, I jumped down through his guards and landed on my feet face to face with my opponent. Always polite, I stuck my hand out to shake his; startled, he jerked back. Once he realized I had no gun, we shook hands and stood there talking. I questioned his actions; Cuomo responded. Meanwhile, the band played the same song over and over, wondering why the speaker of the hour was taking so long to reach the podium.

It was an effective action and great fun, but it could have been better. I learned something that day. When the governor finally arrived at the microphone, he announced he'd been talking to "Mrs. Tissot who asked me a number of things that I will now respond to." He then smoothly proceeded to make up questions suited to his own political agenda. I'd been had! I had failed to prepare handouts for the press with the real questions.

I was raised to shun publicity. In my parents' world, it was considered a cheap stunt for getting attention, a stunt below our station in life. Joining my first protest back in the late '60s had taken all my courage. Did I think protests would be effective? I wasn't sure. What a protest represented for me was the courage to stand up for my convictions. If I dared not show the world what I believed, would those beliefs be real? I still protest when I can.

I did not limit my environmental involvement to politics but volunteered with Pete Seeger's Hudson River Clearwater organization. Along with others, I met busloads of school children at various points along the shores of the river. We brought nets, microscopes, aquariums and books. In tall hip-waders, we shuffled into the river, casting the nets to catch fish for studying. We also cleaned up trash and talked about the importance of recycling. Each day would end with a picnic and songs sung to banjos and guitars. What joyous times those were.

Other occasions for environmental work included participating in an annual study of the wood frog populations. These frogs sing only for two weeks in the early spring when ice still covers part of the vernal pools where they come to mate. Locations can vary, so finding them is a challenge. We would tramp through the leafless April woods, ears cocked to catch their songs that sound much like ducks quacking. Ever since that day, seeking out the song of the wood frog has become an early spring ritual for me.

At times, I joined a large number of scientists, naturalists and volunteers to carry out a bioblitz. This requires taking an inventory, usually over a 24-hour period, of all forms of life in a specified area. It involves netting fish, colleting mud from the bottom of rivers and ponds, using microscopes to study life forms, listing all mosses, plants, mushrooms and trees, tracking wildlife and observing butterflies and birds. It is a real eye-opener. No one could ever use the term "vacant land" after experiencing such a study.

CHAPTER 17

Hitting Bottom?

By 1984, our landlord had become such an unbearable nuisance that we decided to move again. I had always been fascinated by the design of trailers – known euphemistically as mobile homes. We found one in a beautifully kept park. It was located next to a three-acre pond with woods across the way. The compact interior, 12 feet by 70 feet, reminded me of the fun challenge of living on a schooner during the wonderful annual sailing trips made in my youth. Here was something we could afford and so we bought it. The stigma of residing in a trailer park caused some sputtering from Wim but he also saw the humor in it. We had two bedrooms, two bathrooms, a kitchen and a dining/living room. True, it was necessary to literally walk across the top of the coffee table to go from one end of our abode to the other, but that was a minor inconvenience. We even had some friends who sneaked pink, plastic flamingoes into our front yard so we would feel more at home.

We were now paying less than for a rental; owned our own home to remodel as we liked; had a lovely yard with a great weeping willow tree; a pond-side location; a porch for outdoor dining and just 100 yards away, access to acres of hiking and ski trails. The hell with prestige – I loved it. This move did require weeding out our possessions. Our children took some things, the rest we gave away to others in greater need. Learning to manage on a smaller scale was a good challenge and right in line with my goal of living more simply. Trailer parks can be a great solution for those facing a housing crisis, unless located in Tornado Alley.

On first moving in, I was delighted to see that other tenants kept their blinds closed. This meant ours could stay open – letting in sun and starlight without privacy worries. Diana, the occupant of the trailer on the far side of our yard, had been away when we arrived. Upon returning, she immediately opened her blinds, preferring like us, to look out on the beautiful pond and lush woods. This, and the fact we both had large sun-bleached, driftwood sculptures in our front yards was promising. We first met her when she was sunbathing the day after returning from a trip with her boss to Europe. She had told colleagues she was vacationing in Florida and was madly trying to obtain a last minute suntan so her pale skin would not betray her. That clinched it; we liked her immediately.

It was the start of a long and wonderful friendship. We skied, walked, biked, skated on the pond and shared many fine meals together. We looked after her cats when she was away; she looked after Polo when we were away. Being single, she sometimes answered ads and went out on blind dates. When doing so, she would prop a sign in her kitchen window alerting us where she was going and that if she wasn't home by a certain time, to call the police. Isn't that what neighbors are for? We had many good times and laughs, such as the time she was taking a shower and sang happy birthday out the stall window to Wim who was sitting on our porch.

Eventually, Diana bought a house and moved into town. We also moved – but within the park to a double-wide. We got a big kick out of a country western song released at the time: *Me and my bride in the double-wide!* It was a lovely, tan, wood-sided bungalow with three bedrooms (to accommodate visiting family), a large eat-in kitchen, a dining/living room (large enough to dance in) with sliding glass doors opening onto a private backyard surrounded by hedges and bordering the pond. We added a porch roof and spent a good deal of time outside watching the wildlife on the water and in the woods across the way. I got into some trouble with the park owners when I filled our garden with locally transplanted wildflowers. The management, under the mistaken impression that native plants are weeds, wanted us to pull them all out. Fortunately, I won that battle.

It was a safe rural neighborhood; nobody locked doors. That turned out to be a mistake. One afternoon, I was high up in a cottonwood tree behind our house trying to secure a wire from which to hang a birdfeeder. I was startled to see our retired neighbor Walter slink around the corner of the house next door while the occupants were away at work, take a quick look in either direction (but not up) and enter their back door. A few minutes later he emerged with a bottle of wine in hand and raced back home. I laughed so hard I nearly fell out of the tree. Clearly that was not the only house Walter had been raiding. For months, the level of wine in our own bottles always seemed lower than it should have been. Sometimes the bottles would just disappear. We argued about which of us had finished it off. Wim accused me of sneaking drinks. I accused him. To think, all the time it had been Walter – who was also likely backwashing in our supply.

Walter's wife constantly nagged him about his drinking, but Walter got his revenge. It was a cold winter day and had snowed heavily. Over the roar of the plow, we heard a faint cry for help. Rushing outside, we looked all around but could see nothing until I heard, "Up here, I'm up here." Walter's wife had climbed on the roof to shovel off the snow.

Seeing his chance, Walter removed the ladder, went inside and was happily indulging in his beverage of choice. He was extremely annoyed at us for rescuing her.

One drawback to living in trailers is their vulnerability to wind. In 1953, when I was 12 years old, I had been sitting reading at our Brooks Pond cabin when I looked up to see an ominous green sky, unlike anything I had ever seen before. It was so terrifying that I ran to my mother and woke her from her nap (something I was forbidden to do except for dire emergencies). She saw the look on my face and quickly got up. We went down to the boat dock to look around. Behind us, in the direction of Worcester, a large towering white mushroom cloud rose high in the sky. "I think the city has been bombed," she said. It was not a bomb but pretty close. It was a tornado, later classified as an F-4, and it had killed 94 people, injured nearly 1,300 and left 10,000 homeless. I was glued to the radio for days after as they tried to reconnect families. "We have a 5-year-old blond-haired, blue-eyed child with freckles and a mole on her right arm at Memorial Hospital. If anyone knows who she is, please contact us at..." Those were the kind of continuous announcements issued for several days. My brothers volunteered to help with the cleanup and had grisly stories to tell of searching for babies sucked out of parents' arms and bodies under debris. A family that lost everything stayed in our city house in Worcester. Though I had been some 20 miles away from there when the storm hit, the accounts of death and destruction left me traumatized.

Now we were living in what was deemed a "Tornado Magnet." Forget that the Northeast is not subject to tornadoes. It is. Maybe not as many as in Tornado Alley, but they were happening here and increasingly so because of climate change. If fact, one did pass by right off the end of our trailer park. I did not sleep nights when the wind blew hard, in fact had to fight down the fear which, at times, threatened to overwhelm me. With but a modest income and reduced housing options, we, like others in similar circumstances, had to gamely accept the risks.

Among our friends were Doug and Nancy McBride. I first met her in the morning when hiking with Polo. Nancy also enjoyed an early jaunt before going to work. We walked together for a year, sharing our mutual love of birds and plants, before deciding we should have a meal and invite our husbands along. When I told Wim, he asked the name of my friend. I had no idea. Who needed a name? Nobody else was around at that hour of the day. Neither of us, immersed in the crisp dawn of birdsong and wildflowers, had ever thought to ask.

The McBrides became wonderful friends. We enjoyed many martinis and meals together at each other's homes or at The Painter's Tavern in

Cornwall. Once we all made a memorable paddle on the Hudson River that flows between the high cliffs of the Hudson Highlands. We stopped to explore Bannerman's Island where tall ghostly castle ruins still soared into the sky. It was posted land, but we chose to overlook that detail. Nobody occupied it anymore. Munitions had at one time been stored there when the owner, an arms dealer, and his wife had lived in this isolated spot. We found paved overgrown winding paths through gardens of lovely flowers gone wild, and a barely discernible narrow stone staircase descending to the water inscribed with "Steps to Wee Bay," It was achingly romantic, reminding us of our days at De Drommedaris. The island was said to be infested with rattlesnakes, but we figured that was a rumor to keep people away. However, when in the middle of the ruins, I found myself standing not on solid ground but on a thin layer of leaves concealing rusted rebar above a deep, dark chamber below, it occurred to me that perhaps that was where the rattlesnakes were waiting. I exited the premise in a hurry.

We often paddled the majestic Hudson, at times exploring Constitution Marsh, a wildlife refuge. The shores of the river were covered by deep woods with nettings of green vines reaching to the tops of the trees. It seemed tropical in places. Hilly areas alternated with beautiful reed-filled marshes hosting muskrats and ducks. Further down the river by Cornwall-on Hudson and Cold Spring, steep mountains rose straight up channeling the water into a narrower passage.

A stranger had told me what fun it was to kayak-surf the wake of the barges that frequently barreled down the center channel. Great idea, I naively thought. So one sunny day when Wim and I saw a huge empty barge flying along, I said, "See ya'" and headed out to meet my destiny. He and other rational paddlers headed for shore. Just before the wake hit, I looked back to see they had pulled their boats high above the waterline and were standing there watching.

The barge rumbled by and the first wave hit, thrusting me down its slope; then the second picked me up and skidded me along. Lovely. The third wave was my nemesis. It raised me high, then shot me all the way down to the bottom of the river. I managed to surface again, gasping for breath as the wake rolled my boat over and over. I was finally able to bail from the cockpit. A few more waves tossed me up on the shore like a rag doll. After it was ascertained I was still breathing, the laugher started – the others, not mine nor Wim's. He was annoyed at my risking such a crazy maneuver. While lying there, catching my breath, I wondered about the same thing.

CHAPTER 18

Stepping Out on Their Own

In 1987, Christopher and Jennifer got married in a lovely outdoor ceremony at her parents' beautiful New Hampshire farm. It was a good match except for the family fortunes. The ceremony took place on the lawn, a tall grass field in the background, the lovely bride and handsome groom framed by a view of the mountains. Just before the ceremony began, a pileated woodpecker flew over the assembled guests who all responded immediately by looking up and identifying the bird. It said something important about the new family and friends Christopher was acquiring: people tuned into their surroundings.

Earlier, Christopher had dropped out of college. He was going to have to borrow another $5,000 (in addition to the $5,000 he had already borrowed) just to continue. That was a lot of money in those days. He was concerned that he wouldn't be able to pay it all back. What he told *us*, however, was that he just wasn't very interested in the studies and didn't want us to put more money into his schooling. We accepted his explanation. After first working for Burns and Roe, an engineering company, he moved on to a couple of plastics factories before eventually joining a construction company in Vermont where Jennifer was pursuing a Master's Degree in Social Work at a branch of Adelphi University in Burlington.

Meanwhile, Martha had finished high school a year early, despite being threatened with flunking because we didn't own a TV (One teacher insisting she must have one to complete her homework assignments). She was accepted at Western State College (now Western State Colorado University) in Gunnison, CO. To celebrate, she had requested a large radio/tape player. We bought her the best we could afford. At her graduation party, it was stolen. She was heartbroken. This time I did interfere, calling the mothers of several students and telling them that it was her big present from us. We could not afford to replace it. Two days later, the radio was returned to her school locker, restoring her and our faith in good neighbors and small village life.

At sixteen, being quite independent, Martha made her own travel arrangements to go to college, telling us that all we needed to do was deliver her to the plane. We did that, amidst tears at her departure. Three days later we received a postcard from the Raleigh-Durham airport reading: "Oops! Love, Martha." She had boarded the wrong plane. The airline crew had failed to notice the mistake.

In the following years, Christopher and Jennifer moved to Saranac Lake, NY in the heart of the Adirondack Park wilderness. Jennifer's first job was as a social worker for a private elementary school. After Lillee was born, she became the social worker for three public elementary schools. The students knew her as Miss Jenn. She could not walk down the street without children running up and throwing their arms around her. Christopher, after five-and-a-half years with local contractor, Pete Torrance, started his own company, Tissot Construction. With no financial backing, he turned it from a shaky start-up to a fast growing and successful business.

Martha graduated from college and continued on to earn masters and PhD degrees in cardiovascular and pulmonary physiology. In 1994, she married Howard Seim, an accomplished professor and veterinary surgeon at Colorado State University, Fort Collins. We flew out for the wedding, held at a dude ranch. The ceremony took place in a field, an aisle marked on either side with wildflower-filled wine coolers that I had made for the occasion. That was too much temptation for the resident horses. Just before the ceremony began, they came pounding in from another meadow to feast on those delicious blossoms. The Best Men, all veterinarians, jumped up, confronted the horses, slapped them on their rumps and caused them to rear up on their hind legs, whinny wildly and flee back from whence they came. That was effective for about a half-hour when in the middle of the vows, we once more heard thundering hoofs, and back they galloped. Everything stopped while they were again confronted and sent dashing away. Nothing can authenticate a western style wedding like a good old stampede. The rest of the wedding went off without a hitch. Martha looked lovely in a long, white bridal gown. The guests came dressed in everything from dungarees to tuxedos. Wim appeared in red suspenders and walked Martha down the aisle, zigzagging around horse poop. I was assigned to escort their dog to the event.

Shortly after their marriage, Howard voiced concerns about Martha's remaining student debt, wondering why we weren't paying it off. "You married her, she's yours now," we replied. As it turns out, prior to marrying Howard, Martha had managed to save money and pay down a good portion of her loan. She did it by living out of her car or tent while working summers. Sometimes she also managed to find jobs that provided housing. After graduating, she eventually ended up at the University of Colorado, Denver, where she rose to the rank of Associate Professor, running her own lab, researching and teaching.

CHAPTER 19

The Dutch Side of the Family

Throughout our marriage, Oma and Opa Tissot carefully saved their money so they could visit us every few years, usually for a month or more. It took me a long time, however, to understand what a cultural shock these visits were for my in-laws. Our children, unlike their Dutch counterparts, had a lot of freedom, running wild in Wim's parents' eyes. In retrospect, I think they were right. My guidelines for our kids were the same as those my dad had given us at Brooks Pond: you can do whatever you want as long as you don't bother other people. My in-laws were alarmed by our child raising methods, but Oma was loving and kind with Christopher and Martha. Thanks to all their visits, as well as those of Wim's sisters and spouses, the children grew up strongly aware of the Dutch side of their family. They remain interested in their Dutch heritage to this day.

The Tissot van Patot (our official last name) family history is worth noting. Wim's father, Opa, was born in the Dutch Indies (now Indonesia) and sent back to Holland at the age of 19 to earn an engineering degree. He was hovered over and pushed through his studies by his father who retired early and moved to Delft. His real interest was never in engineering but in track and field to which he devoted all his free time. He was a well-known sports writer, sports reporter and coach, staying active until he was 85 years old.

Oma also grew up in the Dutch Indies tropics where life moved slowly, servants waited on the colonials' every need and socializing was a major occupation. She moved back to Holland in her mid-teens. She had grown up with a father who was abusive toward her mother until they finally divorced. Opa and Oma first met aboard ship while traveling to the Netherlands on family furloughs (the usual 6-month leave for Dutch civil servants in the Indies). Soon after Opa finished his studies, they married. I believe they sometimes felt displaced and missed the Dutch Indies.

Wim was born in 1939. He turned one on May 10, 1940, the very day Hitler invaded the Netherlands and subsequently occupied the country for five years. Life for residents was not only depressingly hard but terrifying. Soldiers closed off streets, making unexpected raids on residences in an attempt to round up men and ship them off to German work camps. Wim and his little sister Anny would hide in the backyard sandbox in total fear. Hiding men from these razzias as they were called, was not always successful, though in Wims's father's case it worked. Not only did the Germans take away men, they took away blankets and anything else they needed. In the last year of the war, the hunger beast constantly gnawed at everyone's heels. Wim and his sister trailed their mother around begging for food. She made a few three-day trips on a wooden-wheeled bicycle to work farmers' fields in exchange for some potatoes and cabbages. To keep warm, the family moved to the second floor of the house that could more easily be heated by their small stove. In order to stay even warmer, the children were encouraged not to get out of bed until late in the day. There were fighter-plane dogfights over the heath next to them, and bombers flying overhead. During that last year of the war, known as the *hongerwinter*, over 20,000 Dutch died of starvation.

What does all this do to people? It takes a toll, and that toll does not stop at one or even two generations. His mother became timid and fearful. His father, unhappy with his job at Phillips Electronics Corporation, escaped into sports and spent little time with the family. I wish I had understood all this in my younger years. I was impatient with Oma – unaware of the devastating effects of war. I later learned that she was afraid even of me. Fortunately, before she died, I became wiser, closer to her and much more tolerant. It also helped me understand Wim better. Knowing your partner's past as well as that of his or her parents can go a long way towards a good relationship.

CHAPTER 20

End of a Pottery Career

I spent 11 delightful years producing *Tissot Pottery*. Jeanne and Felix became good friends. My business thrived on a national wholesale level with occasional retail thrown in. Perhaps it thrived too much. Days started at 5 AM when I would make breakfast, take Wim to the train, hike with the dog, then go to work until 6:00 PM. After some years of this, the burden of filling orders began to feel like a chain around my neck. Every week was a race to meet deadlines.

I had intended to produce functional and affordable pottery, items designed for everyday use in cooking, eating and dining. I wanted to contribute toward a culture in which beauty, art, and craftsmanship would conspire to create functional, affordable items for cooking and dining – not art pieces for shelf display. I felt that the manner in which a customer used my wares was a creative collaboration between the two of us.

My pieces were hand built or created on the potter's wheel. They were decorated in a variety of colored glazes depicting flowers, plants, animals, birds, and shells. With some I worked designs right into the clay, producing an earthy textured feel. Despite good intentions, in order to make a profit, my prices had to rise. My customer base changed from true lovers of pottery to well-heeled women who, through boredom, spent their time annually redecorating their houses. I was conflicted by the irony of gaining this kind of buyer.

The demand for matching pieces grew as they were added to collections and wedding registries. I had to make the same designs over and over: dinner sets, casseroles, pitchers, multitudes of bowls, pie pans and mugs, etc. Keeping up with re-orders for earlier pieces and at the same time creating new lines, became increasingly difficult. Multiply ten different decorations times forty different items and one can understand the complexity of it all. The demands of marketing and shipping plus throwing and decorating upwards of 140 pots a week was labor intensive. The pace of production was killing my creativity and wearing me down. Friends suggested I switch to molds or jigs but then the wares would lack the warm and personal character of hands-on work.

I looked for a new way to earn income. When I eventually switched to another job, I was fortunate to find a lovely smaller studio in my friend Linda's barn. I continued to do clay work in my free time but no longer produced for the market. The signature on my pieces changed from a stamp with my name to a pair of wings symbolizing my rediscovered creative freedom. I once more enjoyed the pleasure of sinking my hands into clay, relishing the fleeting beauty of still wet, freshly formed pots, and leisurely producing one of a kind pieces. However, after 2 years, the space was needed for other purposes. I packed up my studio once more, tears streaming, and put everything in storage. I realized I would most likely never make pottery again. I did not realize that writing, equally creative and rewarding, would one day replace it.

The Nefarious World of Business

In 1994, I found a new job as Director of Development for a local natural history museum that had recently acquired a large property. They were in desperate need of funding. With my marketing experience and dedication to preserving the environment, I was enthused about jumping into the work. It seemed a perfect fit. I doubled the general membership and tripled the corporate membership in the first four months. I held frequent wine and cheese parties to show off the newly acquired property and seek donations. But jealousy raised its shaggy head. Staff at the museum (I was located in a distant building) reported that the administration was conspiring to undermine my accomplishments. They stole liquor from the supply for fundraising parties then accused me of spending too much on beverages. They withheld phone calls and information pertinent to my job. Finally, in a deliberate move to humiliate me, the director demanded I call a new corporate member and cancel a major lunch party (planned with his full backing) to be held the next day at the museum. Instead, he had decided to hang an art exhibit in the meeting space at that time. I refused and suggested he make the call. I was fired. That was in1993. Kicking leaves.

After that, the days were dark and long. I knew I had skills as good as any of the managers I had worked under but though I sent out numerous resumes, none resulted in an interview. This was in the early 90's when employment opportunities were starting to dry up. I got a healthy dose of what so many later suffered as their jobs were outsourced and their skills deemed superfluous. It is seriously demeaning to go from an accomplished member of the workforce to being tossed, so to speak, on the trash heap. Subject to periods of depression, I had days that were some of my worst ever. Age worked against me as well, as it does today for so many. It was a deeply humbling time. I had fallen into the category of those who, whether for age, race, gender, disability or other non-rational excuses, endure the painful insult of prejudice. That experience

113

helped me to a deeper understanding of all those who daily suffer from, and must live with, discrimination. So maybe it was a good experience after all.

A few months after that, I found employment with a headhunting firm, hiring doctors for hospitals in the Northeast. It was a difficult job that required cold calling emergency rooms where, more often than not, we were met with angry hostility. No wonder – we were trying to steal their doctors. However, somewhat to my shame, I was pretty successful and promoted to manager of the department. That was not as liberating as one might think. Above me was a blatantly unethical supervisor for whom the end always justified the means. His motto was: get the other guy before he gets you. He believed that everyone was out to scam everyone else. He even managed to exploit the CEO, extracting money from him to fund his personal life. If folks got cheated, my boss explained, it just showed they were dumb and deserved it. I came to understand a lot from this man about the underside of American business and culture.

Hospitals did not welcome our recruiting raids and threatened us with dire consequences if we ever called again. However, the job required we continue doing so. This forced us to constantly change our names. When we received callbacks from interested doctors, it became confusing trying to remember who was working under which alias. I devised a system to keep track of it all. I had one team member assume only fish surnames, another tools, another trees and so on. It injected a little fun into what was pretty miserable work. A phone request would come in for Pam Fish and we would imagine pan fish, glassy-eyed white creatures flopped in a skillet, but we would also immediately know who to give the phone to. Other times it would be for Mary Hammer, or Sally Oak or Sue Otter. We worked within cubicles set into a larger medical company and our conversations, often overheard, gave rise to such loud laughter we had a hard time carrying out the deception with the doctor on the other end of the line.

The arrogance of our supervisor and the disdain he showed us was second to none. So, it was with great delight I entered the office kitchen one day and found him standing in his shiny suit and brogues on top of the dining table whimpering in terror because a mouse was cruising around the floor. "Don't tell anyone," he pleaded, "just get it out of here." Was he kidding? My darker side emerged. I called the office staff to come witness the spectacle. After we all had a good laugh, a couple of us took the mouse outside. Principles failed me again. I enjoyed the sweet revenge. That was not the last.

Another time he asked me to pick him up at Walmart where he was taking his car for an oil change. "I'm so sorry," I told him, "but I don't go to Walmart." I explained about their exploitation of employees, their practice of devastating local commerce and how they drove down salaries in surrounding towns. He asked and got an earful. When I was finished, he just repeated,

"Pick me up at Walmart! I don't care what you think." My boss, my job. I picked him up. When I drove into the parking lot in my VW Vanagon, in order to remain incognito, I put a brown paper bag over my head with cut-out slits for my eyes. He was horrified, got in the car and huddled under the dashboard in fear of being recognized. I almost hit another car on my way out, but it was all so worth it. He never asked me again.

It was on this job that I first learned to use computers. It required hours of my staying after work, trying to figure them out, but the effort was worth it. The computer age was well launched and those who could not, or would not, jump aboard were destined to be left behind.

Saying Goodbye

In 1996, I was visiting my parents when my disoriented dad called me to his bedside. As late as in his seventies, he had rebuilt his entire workshop and two garages by himself after they burned down in a fire. He had rigged a pulley to bring a rocking chair up to the roof so he could enjoy well-deserved breaks from his work. His stamina had been amazing. However, that all ended sometime in his eighties when depression set in. He took to his bed, remaining there for several years while becoming more and more confused. Suddenly, on this particular day, his mind cleared and he said to me, "You know, you should really sell the cabin (his other lake house). Your mother doesn't want to let it go – tells me it would be like cutting off her right arm." I told him I had many wonderful memories of the years enjoyed there, that those would always be part of me. But, I could understand why the cabin should be sold. It was costly to hang on to and none of us children could afford to keep it as a vacation house. He understood, even smiled, then said, "Tell me what you would like to have from this home."

Until bedridden, he'd been a brilliant Thoreau-type individual, content to garden his land, design and build houses, boats and sundials. He loved working in his woodshop where he produced simple rustic pine furniture, as well as carved birds. His motto for everything, which I adopted, was that in design, form should follow function. In some ways, we were quite similar. I told him I would like to have a folk carving he had made of a bird called a black skimmer: black and white, with long orange legs and bill. That delighted him. He cried and I cried. We knew it was our goodbye. Then he zoned out. We were never able to communicate again. He died later that year.

CHAPTER 21

Frying Pan into the Fire

My headhunting job paid well but ran counter to my ethics. It left me anxious to move on. Next I found a manager's position with a nonprofit organization that contracted with New York State to enroll uninsured children into the free *Child Health Plus Program,* an initiative of Governor Mario Cuomo in 1990. It seemed a worthy cause. I was hired to open a branch office in rural Sullivan County some 90 miles north of the headquarters, find the parents of children lacking healthcare and enroll them.

This job required giving public presentations and doing outreach. Bringing uninsured kids into the free program was rewarding. I had a small office with three employees. The number of children we enrolled far exceeded expectations. Big mistake. A woman in a corporation should *never* exceed the boss's expectations, especially if he is male. Our relationship started to unravel. This nonprofit, like so many others, was nevertheless extremely profitable for management. I was so well paid that one year I turned down my holiday bonus. It was an arrogant gesture, but my salary was grossly out of proportion with those of lower ranked employees who worked harder than I did. This did not go over well.

After several months, the CEO asked me to set up a new provider relations department at the headquarters. Being boosted up to a position equal to my boss's did not endear me to him either. I spent several months on this project, asking those in other divisions of the company to tell me in what ways this new department would be of use to them. At first they were reluctant to speak up, fearing retribution from the top. I assured them their names would not be revealed and finally they opened up. When the project was finished, I presented it to the CEO. The first thing she asked was who had made which suggestion. I explained that put me in a difficult spot as I had promised confidentiality to those interviewed. She responded by saying something to the effect that if I was not prepared to rat on folks, I was not fit to join the top ranks of the company. I was to have been put in charge of the new department. No more. They adopted my plan but sent me back to the Sullivan County office.

My boss had told me that, due to the distance of my location, I was not always expected to attend departmental management meetings at headquarters. Nevertheless, I tried to go when I could. The meetings turned out to be a waste of time. The same problems were discussed, the same solutions suggested and nothing ever implemented. One day I left a message with him suggesting there was little point in my coming again until he and I could get together and effect some change. When could we do that? Kicking leaves.

Using that message as an excuse, he tried to fire me for insubordination. The CEO intervened by suspending me for two weeks instead, forbidding me to phone my workers for any reason – which I did immediately – and sending me to a psychiatrist. I was good friends with a major civil rights lawyer. Of course I went to him rather than a psychiatrist, explaining that I felt as if I'd been sent to the Gulag.

"You have," he said and went on to explain this had become a popular corporate tactic for suppressing anyone who chose to speak up. He wrote a letter to the company that guaranteed, for legal reasons, they could never fire me. I stayed on for another year but then decided, due to the toxic environment, it was time to leave.

CHAPTER 22

Suddenly – Grandparents

Within a short period of time, we had acquired four wonderful grandchildren: Christopher and Jennifer were parents to a girl, Lillee, born in 1991 and a boy, Braxton, born in 1993. Martha and Howard had Miranda, born in 1995 and Howie, born in 1998. We visited the Colorado family when we could, which was not often enough, making the trip by car and camping along the way. We had often camped with our children, believing those expeditions would bring us all closer to nature and the realization that happiness can be found outside the material world. To our delight, both families continue to enjoy the outdoors: camping, climbing, hiking, skiing, snowboarding, biking, and paddling.

We managed to see Christopher's and Jen's family (who lived five hours away in Saranac Lake) more often than Martha's family in Colorado. But, due to job restraints, we weren't able to see either of them as often as we would have liked.

One year, Martha asked me to come to Colorado and take care of their two children, 3-year-old Miranda and 18-month-old Howie, so she and her husband could make a month long kayak trip through the Grand Canyon. Up against work deadlines, I had earlier turned down a request from Christopher and Jen to help out when their family was sick. I felt terribly guilty about that so when Martha asked, I said "sure." I imagined, now that I was a grandma, my temper would have mellowed, giving away to the blessed patience of age. It didn't work out quite like that.

Miranda and Howie were adorable and sweet tempered until they saw their parents pulling out of the driveway. Then, like the family dog, they tried to chase the car. I had a hard time holding them back. Up until that day, Martha had been nursing Howie. I was tasked with suddenly weaning him. It made for some challenging weeks.

Miranda was enrolled in a Waldorf preschool where I dropped her off each morning. However, she would not remain quietly there until I entertained her whole class by doing cartwheels in front of the windows. Why her parents ever started that tradition I didn't know. What I did know was that grandma's cartwheels gave rise to a good deal of mirth among teachers and kids alike. What we won't do for the next generation. It was an exciting month with many ups and downs that sorely tried my patience but also a wonderful chance for me to bond with two adorable grandchildren.

Several times over the years, we drove out west to see our Colorado family, camping and taking our bikes for side trips along the way. These trips added greatly to our knowledge of the many different cultures thriving within our borders which are frequently overlooked by the coastal communities. Eventually, Christopher and Jen built a lovely vacation house near Driggs, ID directly across from the Grand Tetons. This new destination was added to our itinerary.

Highlights of these excursions included: the Christmas we spent with Martha's family; a weekend ski trip to a Colorado back country yurt (followed by my contracting giardia); and the 50th anniversary trip the children generously gave us during which we stayed at Christopher and Jen's Idaho home, partied with the family and skied cross-country at Yellowstone National Park. We also watched the family powder ski at Grand Targhee by riding in the open back of a specially chartered snow-cat which carried us high up above the lifts to the top of the mountain. It was a straight up and down trip with huge drop-offs beside the trail. Enough excitement for us but not enough for our children and grandchildren all of whom love the thrill of back country off-trail skiing. It was a joy to watch them hurtle down precipitous descents, gracefully slicing through deep powder to leave behind clouds of white dust and intertwining ribbon tracks.

After observing them for a few hours, we were ready to snowshoe to the bottom and warm up. Unexpectedly, the guides forbade this, directing the ski patrol to take us "elderly" down by rescue toboggan. How embarrassing to ride the sled of shame. I limped around trying to at least give the appearance of needing such a lift. We were bundled onto the toboggans and whisked down steep slopes at terrifying speeds until the ski patrol was called for a real emergency. Suddenly our welfare was not so important. They unceremoniously "dumped" us halfway down the mountain, not so concerned after all. We managed the rest of the descent, as originally planned, on snowshoes.

Our extremely generous children were to give us two more trips, both bicycling adventures in Holland. What a thrill to revisit the land where we had first met and now return accompanied by the next generation. The most recent trip, in 2016, started with a 50-year-plus reunion at De Drommedaris where our romance had first bloomed. It had just been beautifully restored and was operated again as a cultural center. Old friends and colleagues from earlier days joined us there to celebrate. Leaving there we ferried across the IJsselmeer and biked in the northern provinces, mostly in Friesland, stopping along the way for meals with friends and family.

On the first day, near Enkhuizen, I managed to run my bike off the path and execute a face-plant on the pavement. Fortunately, despite what I suspect was a broken rib, I was able to get back on my wheels and complete the trip, shored up with Ibuprofen. I blamed it all on the beautiful countryside which distracted me from the task of staying on course. (A frequent dilemma in my life). This last trip was a rugged one that included sleet, snow, and 40-mile-an-hour winds, in late April no less. But we looked at it as a bonding time. What else could we do – and who could ever forget a trip like that? In between the clouds, the sun would burst through onto spectacular views of mast-filled harbors, dikes loaded with sheep, colorful tulip fields stretching into the distance, and charming ancient villages. It was a thrill as well as a distraction. Our last stop was at Wim's sister Anny and her husband Wybo's house. There we had a large and joyous family reunion, complete with a delicious *rijsttafel* (a special Indonesian meal) prepared by Anny, a gourmet chef. Little did we know that would be our last time with her. She died of cancer just nine months later.

Intrusions

I had often been concerned about the invasion of toxic chemicals into our lives in the form of cleaning supplies, cosmetics and toiletries. After leaving my job with Child Health Plus, I began selling supplements and nontoxic cleaning products. That required putting in 14-hour days to make any progress at all. In addition, I would not aggressively pitch a monthly buying plan to folks who I knew could not really afford it. The job became an intrusion into family life and principles.

September 11, 2001, I was driving back from a breakfast meeting with the radio on when I heard a plane had crashed into one of the World Trade Center Towers. How terrible, I thought. Then a few minutes later, when I heard a second plane had hit, I knew it was terrorism – and well beyond terrible. It immediately came to me that, after this invasion into our lives, nothing would ever be the same again.

I rushed home to see Renée, my elderly neighbor. Her son Patrick worked high up in one of the twin towers. By the time I arrived at her door, she had already heard the news. I stayed with her watching TV. She received a call from Patrick's partner who said her son had called and that he reported seeing burning papers falling out of the sky past his office window. Against official security advice to stay put, he was evacuating his entire staff. A reminder: people who are supposed to know, don't always, especially in critical situations.

We sat watching events until suddenly the screen filled with a huge cloud of smoke and dust. "How strange," Renée murmured, "I don't see the towers anymore." Bewildering. After a few minutes, an announcer delivered the fateful news. The Towers had collapsed. In an effort to offer comfort, I told her that Patrick was much too smart to be anywhere near that place. Renée was stoic, never breaking down nor crying. I fixed her lunch while we continued to watch in silence. Three hours later, she got another call. Her son was somewhere on a boat out in the New York harbor. Everyone in his office had safely escaped, thanks to Patrick who had kept a cool head.

One of our friends and a number of New York City firefighters living in our area died. Many others were badly traumatized. We all flew American flags and mourned. It was a grievous time. But when the US invaded Iraq, a country that had nothing to do with this terrorist act – had no weapons of mass destruction according to official inspectors, I took our flag down in protest. To me, invading Iraq was a political move sadistically based on the roiled up emotions of a grieving citizenry. I was roundly criticized by neighbors who declared, "If you're not for the invasion, you're against the USA."

To this I responded, "Blind compliance is not patriotic, speaking up is."

CHAPTER 23

Adirondacks, Here We Come

In 2001, Jennifer asked why we had never thought of moving to Saranac Lake. "You would love it here," she told us. We knew that and had, in fact, often thought of relocating to the north but felt it wasn't fair to pursue them as maybe they had moved in part to establish their own territory away from us.

We had already become attached to the Adirondacks. On visits to see the family, we had often been lured into hiking the lovely woods and mountains. One time I had driven up to see the family, arriving after 2 PM. "What took so long?" Christopher asked? I tried to weasel out of the answer, but he noticed my muddy boots. I was caught. The Northville-Placid trail had beckoned. I had stopped to hike.

On another occasion, after a weekend visit, Wim and I left their place early one Sunday morning to beat the traffic going south as we set out on the long trip home. When we reached Giant Mountain trailhead, the temptation was too much. We parked and headed upwards. Late afternoon found us sitting high up on a cliff overlooking the very road full of traffic we had planned to avoid.

In 2001, Christopher and Jen invited us to come live near them and for me to run the Tissot Construction office. Business had grown fast and he needed someone to organize his administration. I was good at that – though not an inspired bookkeeper. We were delighted. "We'll give you twenty-four hours to retract your offer. If you do not, we will come," I said, in an effort to let them off the hook should they have spoken too quickly. They had not. In February, 2002, with less than a month's notice, I put an end to fifteen years of life in the Hudson Valley, packed the car and headed for Saranac Lake. At age sixty, I moved into a studio apartment in a building owned by Christopher and Jen. I immediately began working for Tissot Construction.

Wim's Trail

In 1976, Wim had left prep school teaching to work at Columbia University's Butler Library in New York City where he made friends, was promoted and generally thrived. Then in 1979, to earn more money, he went to work at the Traffic Bureau of the Netherlands Ministry of

Defense on lower Broadway. With a name like that, you would never expect one of its paychecks to bounce, but on one occasion it did, to my amusement and the bank's surprise. When the bureau moved its American office to Baltimore, Wim spent a couple of years programming an extensive mailing list for the National Foreign Trade Council, along with writing their weekly newsletter. That job completed, he transferred to the H.W.Wilson Company, publisher of the *Readers' Guide to Periodical Literature* and indexer of all the major newspapers and journals. He worked for twelve years at this high pressure job, building up a pension and savings but in 2001, was fired for insubordination, a frequent occurrence in our family. He moved on to a less frantic pace at the New York Public Library. His fluency in several languages was welcome in his new position. His jobs were all intellectual but poorly paid. That was his situation when we decided to leave the overcrowded Hudson Valley.

Caving to Ownership

We put our double-wide up for sale, Wim staying in Orange County until he could find a buyer and land a job in Saranac Lake. Neither endeavor went well. He remained where he was while I lived up north. We had committed to buying a modular, wood-sided, energy efficient chalet built in Canada. Christopher accompanied me to the factory to determine how well the houses were built. He was mightily impressed and helped me customize changes to the blueprints.

Because he owned a building business, he was offered the home at a wholesale price in hopes he would become a representative in the U.S. Afraid to lose the deal if the company realized he was our son but not interested in working with them beyond that, we had kept up a charade during the negotiation process. I pretended he was my contractor, never mentioning his last name. After the factory tour, the salesman turned to Christopher and said, "Do you think this will work for your mother?" Nailed. Though our cover was blown, they still offered the better price.

We had bought a 5.5-acre lot next to the future site of Christopher and Jen's new home: land they had bought as a buffer and then sold to us. Did they really want our house there? They never said no. We assumed it was okay. There was plenty of space. It was a beautiful wooded lot on the back side of Dewey Mountain, an easy 2-mile walk to the village. We kept the house footprint small and opted for no lawn so as not to disturb the forest any more than necessary. Christopher's company installed the driveway, basement, and infrastructure. In June, 2002, the house arrived in two pieces on the back of two trucks. Each looked about the size of a fishing shack. However, once the crane had lifted the two sections onto the basement walls it began to take on larger proportions. After that, the two roof pieces were raised to make a gable, the knee-joists dropped into place and a ridgepole was laid across the top. Christopher, promising a supper of beer and pizza, persuaded his workers to stay late Friday evening to finish up the shingling. By suppertime we had a new home. One of the best parts for me? We had a basement to hide from potential tornadoes or microbursts, rare but not unheard of in the Adirondacks.

I moved in the next day, sleeping on the floor between piles of building material. The interior still needed work, including finishing off the upstairs rooms, but I needed to get in quickly as our funds were running low. Land rent for the double-wide, two mortgages and the apartment rent were putting us in a squeeze. Suddenly, in August when we didn't see how to stretch our money an inch further, everything came together. Our old home sold for a good price and Wim was hired by the Paul Smith's College library. It is said you must take on risk in order to reach your goals. However, if you lose your gamble, folks are quick to condemn your bad judgment. I think success has a whole lot to do with good luck – good luck and calculated risk.

Despite my conviction that ownership tends to insulate folks from the hardships of those less fortunate, we found ourselves now in possession of a delightful, cozy home tucked deep in a maple/beech woods. It was the first real house we had ever owned, but I felt we now came disturbingly close to joining the elites of the world. That idea was quickly dispelled when a nearby resident made the disparaging remark that I couldn't understand the difficulties of buying a new home because we had only purchased a "kit house." And then, to make matters worse, we had the audacity to install a gray mailbox along the road, unlike the black ones erected by our neighbors. We were still, after all, comfortably outside the establishment.

Good Landing

After six months, Wim and I were able to be together again and be near part of our family. We had landed in a good place. He enjoyed his job at Paul Smith's and I liked the challenge of organizing my son's business office. I was reminded of his toddler days when he played with toy trucks and building blocks. Who would have believed where that was to lead?

I was extremely grateful for the job, the opportunity to live in the Adirondacks and the chance to explore the mountains and lakes. I was also delighted not to have to return to the American hard-ass business world. I thought that living in a small wilderness community would be a quiet affair – not so. In addition to spending more time with the family, we found ourselves caught up in a whirl of activity. While Saranac Lake was fast becoming a regional center for the arts, music, literature and theater, it also was (and still is) a town with a large socio-economic divide. While many work hard to right this inequality, hopefully even more can be done to provide all residents with better opportunities to share in the good life.

People understand the importance of biodiversity in nature (Noah saw it first) but that should extend to mankind as well. Unfortunately, racial diversity is lacking in this town. The more people we meet of different color and character, the more we learn how little we have to fear – how much we share in common.

Another Goodbye

A little more than a year after we moved to the Adirondacks, my 97-year-old mother fell ill at her home in Massachusetts. There were no good options for taking care of her there so I brought her up to be with us. Just in time. She was admitted to the hospital with pneumonia and a heart attack; later with a broken hip. Nights I stayed with her, sleeping in her room; days I continued going to work. But, my mother, always active and healthy, in fact still walking the woods and rowing her boat at ninety-seven, survived it all in good shape. However, she was not well enough to return home and live by herself in a rather isolated location, so we rented a small studio apartment for her at Saranac Village at Will Rogers, a beautiful senior living establishment. It had originally been started as the National Vaudeville Artist Lodge, a hospital for professional actors and actresses with lung disease. One of the objectives was to design the building so it would not feel like a hospital but rather a warm, welcoming lodge. In that, the architect succeeded.

At first she found the establishment delightful. But once it was determined she had to remain there, she did not find it so charming anymore. Being a feisty woman and class-conscious, she rebelled at everything, calling residents "inmates" and telling her tablemate she was nothing but a human garbage disposal. The staff was wonderful and patient with her. We were delighted to have such an amazing place where she could live.

For me, having her nearby was a gift. Difficult as she was and as much attention as she required in the seven years she lived there, we became closer, our relationship less formal. It feels good to heal rifts. I wish every family could have a chance to do the same. Wim and I enjoyed dinners and games with her, took her on picnics, shopping trips, to the theatre, to our home and to restaurants. Our children and grandchildren visited her often. Something about being away from her own kingdom had softened Mother. She was a little less controlling, a little less demanding ... but not entirely.

At first, she refused to wear the "Help, help, I've fallen and can't get up" button. After several tumbles to the floor followed by hours of waiting for assistance, she finally complied. We explained it was only to be used for emergencies. Upon stopping by the next day, I learned she had pushed the button, sending the entire staff rushing to her room, only to find she had dropped her jewelry box and needed someone to crawl under the bed and retrieve an earring. The director gave her a talking-to, then actually got down on his hands and knees and did as she wanted.

For Mother's 100th birthday, Christopher and Jen invited a large group of friends and extended family to celebrate at their home – and come they did: from Colorado, Connecticut, Massachusetts, New Hampshire and quite a few from her home state of Virginia. It was an enormous gathering. She was alert, looked beautiful and enjoyed every minute of it.

Mother lived on the second floor of Will Rogers and insisted upon walking up and down the stairs to and from her apartment. She did this until she was 103 years old and had to leave because of confusion. An excellent example of the benefits of keeping fit. She moved in with my brother Henry and his wife Fiona in their Maine home where she received excellent care. My brother Robin had looked after her finances for several years and later, he and his wife, Lana, stayed with her at times so that we could take vacations. She died just three weeks prior to her 106th birthday, beautiful up to the end, leaving us with many fine memories. She was a good storyteller, loved tending her flowers and cross-stitching everything from towels and curtains to baby quilts and tablecloths which she gave to family members. She gave me something else as well. Some years earlier, while we were sitting at dinner, she had said, "Put your hand under the table" I did so and she slipped her diamond ring on my finger. Personal feelings were hard for her to express – she did it that way instead.

CHAPTER 24

Oh Joy, Retirement!

I worked three years for Tissot Construction, before retiring at age sixty-three. During that time, I had come to love the North Country sense of humor, that is until, the joke was on me. I had been adamantly opposed to invading Iraq, protested weekly and had a bumper sticker expressing my opinion on the matter. For the longest time I drove around unaware that one of his guys had crossed out two letters and changed *"Don't send troops to Iraq"* to *"Do send troops to Iraq."* Retaliation was called for. I put a sticker on his truck bumper proclaiming that he was a vegetarian and opposed to hunting: a total humiliation for one who was a backcountry hunter and scorned vegetarians. It was a new truck and the sticker could not be removed without damage. Not only did he get really mad but so did my son. Oh well.

Christopher had an enormously complex business. I was privileged to observe the creativity and skill he brought to it. We don't always get to witness the accomplishments of our grown children. Of Martha's job, for instance, we understood little. We knew that it dealt with the function of cells at high altitude and had earned international respect from others in her field. Beyond that we were at a loss, as is often the case for parents trying to understand the work of the next generation in this fast changing technical world.

I had always dreaded the idea of retirement, thinking I would be shunted aside from an active life. However, after moving to the Adirondacks, I couldn't wait. It was obvious to me that retired people here were in great shape and having a fantastic time enjoying the outdoors, attending local events and volunteering. Part of what makes the town such a culturally active place is all the work volunteers contribute, not only for environmental and cultural organizations but to help the less advantaged as well. One of my first forays into joining this community was by doing a little tour guiding at the Robert Louis Stevenson Cottage. I was surprised, when showing visitors around, how little they knew about Saranac Lake's history as a tuberculosis curing town.

The Writing Plunge

I had often thought of trying my hand at writing, had in fact, through the years, written hundreds of snippets on torn off scraps of paper that lay buried somewhere in my files. Environmental work and jobs had required a number of articles but not the kind I particularly enjoyed doing. I wanted to follow my own instincts, write about my perceptions of events and culture. Inspired by tourists' lack of knowledge about Saranac Lake's history, I set about creating a three-part flier for the local historical association, Historic Saranac Lake (HSL). It was titled: *Before you Leave Here, Find out Where You Have Been.* It was a short summary of the town's history, its importance and why visitors should take the walking tours and read about the area. The flier was adopted by HSL which distributed hundreds of copies before replacing it with an updated version.

Encouraged by this first attempt, I joined a writing group and submitted articles to a few hard copy and online Adirondack journals. To my surprise, they were accepted. About the same time, I had been invited by Jeanne DeMattos, an active community member, to join a group of longtime women residents who had met for lunch once a week for over twenty years at the Hotel Saranac. I felt honored.

One day at lunch, a member of the group, Bea Drutz, said, "Everybody talks of the history of Saranac Lake, but nobody asks us for *our* stories." What an opportunity. I recorded their stories, wrote them down and, to put them in context, interjected local history between the lines. It took 3 years but the book, *History Between the Lines, Women's Lives and Saranac Lake Customs, 2007,* was finally completed, with photographer Mark Kurtz providing portrait photos.

Experience in public speaking helped me market the book. I offered workshops around the region, sharing my experience and encouraging others to save written oral histories. I was also invited by a chapter of the American Association of University Women to talk about women in the workplace. I got a particular kick out of this because, years earlier, I had been told that without a college degree I could not become a member of this august organization.

A writing addict I had become. For a couple of years, I interviewed and wrote stories about residents for our local newspaper, *The Adirondack Daily Enterprise,* but stopped when I needed more time to work on other projects.

Writing my first book was an exhausting undertaking. I swore I'd never publish again. That was not to be. In 2008, I was fascinated to learn how over one hundred volunteers in Saranac Lake come together every winter to build an elaborate Ice Palace, only to see it knocked down less than three weeks later. My first thought was: they are all crazy. My second thought: I want to join them. I did, learning how to break off and pole ice, slush the Palace, load the crane, and other miscellaneous jobs. I was amazed at how much knowledge it took to oversee the construction of such a curious fortress. This brought me to research and write my next book: *Adirondack Ice, a Cultural and Natural History, 2010*. For this book, one of the topics I wrote about but felt I needed to experience to understand, was ice climbing. Why would *anyone* be insane enough to do it?

So, I invited a group of my nine craziest friends, including my son, and hired two professional guides to teach us. The guides paled a bit when they saw how gray-hired some of us were – myself at 69 the oldest of all. They gamely rigged us out with equipment, threw a couple of instructions our way, hooked us to climbing lines and sent us cold turkey up the ice cliff. The climbing itself demands full attention, no time to be afraid of heights – unless you look down of course. It was pretty exciting and pretty scary. I brought a camera with me. One guide offered to suspend me off a tree at the top so I could be lowered in my harness down the vertical cliff wall and get a bird's eye view of the climbers below. It was heart-stopping but I took some pretty cool photos. Afterwards, when I was safely at the bottom again, my climbing harness suddenly fell down around my ankles. The guides were horrified – as was I. It seems that after using the outhouse hours earlier at the beginning of the day, I had not buckled myself in tightly enough. I'm sure they never let that happen again.

What did I take away from this climbing experience? Several things: one is never too old to try something new; it is good to push your limits; overcoming fear is exhilarating; and sometimes to succeed we must put full trust in another person, in this case the one belaying the climbing rope. What I didn't take away was an understanding of why anyone would do this more than once.

After publication of the ice book, I delivered over thirty related power-point presentations around the North Country, eventually becoming so bored hearing myself talk that I stopped. Doing the book circuit, however, provides a venue for getting one's work into the hands of readers. But, as this had been an all consuming project, I vowed it would be my last book.

Yet a year after this venture, I jumped in again, intrigued by the people who work as caretakers for the Great Camps lining our lakes. These jobs, overlooked by the general public, support a good part of the local economy. Curiosity led me to investigate further. I found that in the interest of privacy, caretakers are obligated, if not sworn, to confidentiality about the wealthy and sometimes famous folks they work for. Therefore, to write about their culture, I had to make it fictional and for the most part write only parallel stories that would protect the owners' anonymity. At the same time, I wanted to capture the flavor of their lives. This produced a novel: *Tibetta's World, High Jinks and Hard Times in the North Country, 2012* (A title that will be changed in a later edition).

Along the way, people requested I write specifically about the Carnival's Ice Palace in response to tourists' interest. Titled, *Saranac Lake's Ice Palace, a History of Winter Carnival's Crown Jewel*, 2012, this 54-page, spiral-bound booklet includes a chapter from my *Adirondack Ice* book and was generously sponsored by local businesses and organizations. All profits are donated to the Winter Carnival Committee.

After finishing that book, hoping to improve my writing style, I turned to the beautiful use of language in poetry: the sound and feel of words. I had much to learn and so delved into the subject for a couple of years before writing my own poems. Eventually, I produced two collections: *Adirondack Flashes and Floaters; a River of Verse*, 2014 and *The Beat Within; Poetry, Another Round, 2017*.

Collections are less of a total time commitment than a long book. I would stick with them, I told myself. However, once more, against best intentions, I was drawn back again into writing a full-length book, this time my memoir. I can't imagine there will be more but I'm not promising.

I am only one in a family of several writers, so perhaps it is not surprising that I am drawn by this avocation. In all my endeavors I have been greatly helped by Wim who is not only a good editor but translator as well. My brother-in-law Wybo has also generously donated his formatting skills for a couple of my books. What does writing mean to me? It is a chance to order my thinking, carefully express what I want to say and share my views. My writing also relieves friends and family from the burdensome obligation of listening to me babble about all that runs through my head. My husband disputes that ...

Often I have trouble sleeping, ideas popping up at all hours of the night. I thought when I retired, sleep would improve. Not so. My muse is a night owl fluttering around my head as I lie snuggled under the covers. The only defense? – keep pen and paper nearby, turn on the light and capture the tidbits she drops at my side. Then I chase her away and reenter dreamland. By morning, I have a new stack of material from which to work.

CHAPTER 25

Exploring Near and Far

On arriving in the North Country, we joined the Adirondack Mountain Club. From going with members on outdoor expeditions, we learned much about the area's lakes, mountains and woods. It was a warm and welcoming group. Eventually, we also took to leading outings and, in fact, introduced bicycling as another means of exploring the region. I found that only a few members had much interest in knowing about plants, trees and wildlife. So I bought books, consulted naturalists and undertook my own amateur efforts at identification. The area, having intensely cold winters and filled with mountains and bogs, hosts species unfamiliar to a Massachusetts native. I discovered a whole new world.

During one of our Colorado visits, our daughter, thinking we were experienced river paddlers, took us to the Cache la Poudre River for what she told us was a beginner's ride. "It will give you an adrenaline rush and memories you'll never forget," she announced. "Of course, we'll only be paddling riffles." Ha! No problem, we had often paddled riffles. In fact, I had once joined a kayak rescue team, escorting a swim marathon on a stormy day on Long Island Sound. After that challenge, I *thought* I was ready for anything. Upon arrival at the put-in, we were greeted by a turbulent whitewater river loaded with rocks and flowing in a torrent off the Rocky Mountains. Not our idea of riffles.

Once launched in our rental kayaks, Wim with 8-year-old Howie tucked in front of him and loaded down with provisions and 10-year-old Miranda in front of me, we set off with these instructions: "If you get thrown out of your boat, face downstream and KEEP YOUR FEET UP – if you don't, they'll get caught in the rocks and you'll drown!"

"Oh great! Riffles?"

And from Howard who had just paid a $3,000 bond to rent our equipment, "Whatever you do, *don't* let go of the paddles. It will cost a bundle!" Wim immediately got caught in a strainer (a dangerous low hanging tree branch). Desperately holding on to his paddle caught under water beneath his boat, he had to be rescued. After freeing him, we set off downstream, Martha calling back, "Be sure to avoid the rocks and holes!"

"But Martha, in this turbulence, how can I see rocks and holes?" The answer was swallowed by the roaring river, as was the sight of her kayak.

All I could make out were wild waves breaking and exploding into the air as they hit God knew what on their way to oblivion. On my own now, I saw no reasonable course (reasonable by my standards) as I tried to peer ahead around my granddaughter's helmet. Oh well, I thought, let's just go for it! So we and the river began to pour through one waterfall after another (this description was later disputed by my daughter). "Whoopee," I yelled, holding my paddle aloft in utter surrender as we shot through the rapids, waves cascading over us, flooding and bending the boat into a V shape before flowing out again as the inflatable kayak snapped back into shape. "Wow Miranda, what fun!" I yelled, trying to put a good face on one of the more terrifying experiences I had ever had in all my sixty-six years.

We finally made a picnic stop, but Wim's boat didn't appear for another fifteen minutes. That was worrisome. Did the river get them? Had they both sunk to the bottom of the fearsome rapids? They finally arrived, explaining that their boat, more heavily loaded, had beached on a rocky island. "How did *you* avoid it?" Wim asked resentfully.

"What island?" I said, "There was an island?" Lunch finished, we slithered back into our boats and rushed on. Suddenly, near the planned takeout, Miranda and I sideswiped a large rock and were flung out into the crashing waves. Facing forward as the current tumbled along, I managed to grab the back of her lifejacket.

"Miranda," I shouted over the noise of the river and after several seconds trying to inhale air instead of water, "Keep your feet up!"

"I am, Grandma!" Not only were her feet properly up but she still clutched her paddle. I had mine too. When her daddy speaks, we all listen. In no time, Martha was at our side. Miranda grabbed the stern of her mom's kayak and was quickly dragged to safety.

I, like an autumn leaf, continued a downstream sweep toward the scariest rapids I had seen yet, while Howard, a man who knows his priorities, was busy saving the costly rental boat. With my last ounce of strength, I grabbed hold of a large rock and, still gripping my paddle, collapsed on top like a washed-up fish. My dear daughter returned to pull me to shore. She paddled hard, but to my dismay, it was too much for her and we just weren't moving. Turning around to see why, she burst out laughing. "You have to let go of the rock Mom, I can't pull you and that boulder."

Martha did give us an adrenaline rush and memories we'll never forget, but she still contends they were riffles. I beg to differ. Flat water suits me better. I can relax and take in the wonders of the scenery.

On a quieter note, I continue to pedal my bike (since 2017 on an electric bike), paddle my boat and explore the Adirondacks on foot, skis and snowshoes. Our Dutch family has been heard to mutter, "If you weren't out doing so much, you wouldn't have all those injuries." I laugh and admit the truth to that. But life is short. We love the majesty of the mountains, mystery of the woods and quiet of the lakes. Some risk comes with the territory. I have little desire for safe exercise inside a stifling, sweaty gym. I am lucky to live in the midst of a gorgeous wilderness, beckoning me every day to step out and enjoy its beauty. But other things beckon as well.

So Much Calling Me

With the luxury of free time, writing has become a passion, but there is so much else. I enjoy reading as well, reading being the best training for writing. Wim started a small study group that focuses on fiction. I am an enthusiastic member.

For several years, I ran a lecture series at the Saranac Lake Free Library, started by the same Jeanne DeMattos who had initially invited me to join her lunch group. It was a rewarding endeavor thanks to audience enthusiasm and to the many fascinating people I met: from scientists to authors, naturalists to artists, musicians to performers. But there comes a time when one should voluntarily step down, let new folks take over, and so I did. Nobody is irreplaceable.

In 2015, I took up playing a psaltery, a beautiful southern instrument, handmade by local musician, Charlie Marshall. It is a 24-inch long triangular sound box with thirty fretted strings that are played with a bow. The sound is sweet as a bird's song and sounds a bit like a violin. It is fairly simple to learn – perfect for someone like me with little musical talent. At the age of 9, I had had the audacity to fire my piano teacher. Mother and Dad must have seen how futile the lessons as they never hired her back. I play some piano from sheet music but had wanted to find an instrument I could master well enough to play along with others. The psaltery seemed the answer. I was bolstered in my efforts by what Pete Seeger had said to me in the days when I worked with *Clearwater*. They went something like this: it is better to participate in actively making music than only to listen, even if you can't play very well. His words were the permission I needed. When I play music, the rest of the world drops away.

Wim is a lovely piano player. The two of us get together evenings to practice duets. Other times we join a small group of musicians for a few hours of fun as well. Playing the old songs reminds me of one of the great honors of my life – which I managed to miss. The summer I worked at Mystic Seaport, I went out with a Yale man who was one of the famous *whiffenpoofs*, the a cappella singing group. He and his fellow *Whiffenpoofs* serenaded me late one night at the boarding house where I was staying. Unfortunately, I was taking a bath and didn't hear a thing. However, my landlady did. She called the police, unaware that folks actually paid money to hear those guys sing.

And finally there is now more free time for family. We stay in frequent contact with children and grandchildren, playing wild doubles Ping-Pong and exploring the outdoors. We also enjoy more contact with my brothers and their wives. They say the death of parents will either break up siblings or unite them tighter than before. I am happy to say we are part of the latter group. There were bumps along the way but in the interest of taking care of our aging parents, disposing of the family properties, and giving each other moral support, we came together. Harmony involves effort on everyone's part, but good family relationships are well worth the effort.

CHAPTER 26

Learning Curve

My dreams often include the rugged peaks of China, a place I've never seen. I've read novels set there and seen photos our children and grandchildren have taken when traveling in the Far East. But I have no idea why I dream of such a place. As I grow older, in fact, I have little idea why anything is the way it is. I now see that much of the culture surrounding me is based on the collective acceptance of arbitrary assumptions: politics, manners, lifestyles, religions. It is by tacitly agreeing with these assumptions, or stories, that we function as a society. To question them, to wonder if they are valid, as I do, is to place myself on the fringes of that society.

Because of our insignificance in the scope of a mysterious universe, it is silly to get riled up over the small stuff. I am learning not to but running out of time. As the saying goes: "God grant me patience – but hurry." I've learned a lot from our children about not sweating the minor things, staying positive and laughing. Sometimes I even *remember* those lessons.

For instance: Wim and I once stopped for a picnic on a beautiful large rock on the edge of a quiet lake in Harriman State Park. A couple with children approached and plunked themselves down beside us. I was annoyed. With all the wild land available, why did they have to crowd in on our spot? Years later, I sat with Christopher, Jennifer and the grandchildren, again on a rock by a lake, this time in the Adirondacks. A noisy family came along and asked if they could sit with us. "Of course," Jennifer answered, "there's room for all. We don't own the rock." Giving in to the small things brings its own rewards – a good reason to share.

Another time Martha was driving in Queens, NY. I sat in the front, with the two grandchildren in car seats in the back. Not only were we lost and running late, but we were caught up in a horrendous traffic jam. I was visibly and verbally exasperated with everything: poor traffic management, overcrowding, climate change (it was hot), lousy road designs and life in general. Martha leaned over and whispered, "If *you* get upset, the *children* get upset. If *we* stay calm, they stay calm." She was so right. Patience is the better way – something I try to practice but with difficulty. *Please God, hurry.*

Retirement is a great leveler. Friendships are based on shared interests rather than on past positions in the working world. I find I enjoy people a lot better than when I had to work with them. Have I softened, or have they? I fear the competitiveness of the job world, promoted by capitalists as a virtue, in fact brings out the worst in mankind.

Our Dutch relatives who often crossed the sea to visit used to comment, "Americans are so frantic, always rushing around. Why not just sit and have another cup of coffee?" And why not? Often because employees in this country, worked to the bone, have little time for anything else – like home, family and recreation. There is no safety net. Injury or illness can lead to the loss of everything. Fear keeps folks with their noses to the grindstone. until they are lucky enough to retire. Then – that second cup will be filled, not only with coffee, but with a joyful sigh of relief.

Though we have made several wonderful trips with our children, we have little desire to travel more than that. Our co-retirees cast pitying looks our way, believing, no doubt, that we are wasting our lives. However, we find plenty to fill us with wonder right here in the Adirondacks: a misty dawn full of birdsong; a frigid winter day, the air filled with sun-sparkling crystals; tall, lanky trees bowing to the power of wind; a raft of black and white loons gathered on a blue autumn lake; the fright and awe of a thunderstorm; the hoot of an owl in the dark of night; a flaming fall forest at the foot of snow covered mountains.

There is much to be learned from books, but also to be learned from our local artists, performers, musicians, and writers. I've come to realize that whether someone makes it to the top depends more on luck, marketing and self-promotion than on skill. Many of our folks never receive the widespread recognition they deserve. Supporting them here in our own area is important. These people, many highly accomplished, help us see more views of life than there are mice in the Adirondacks.

Volunteer Conundrum

If you so much as stick a toe in the volunteer waters of any small town, you will quickly be sucked into a whirling vortex of commitment. Since the children moved away I have devoted a part of my life to volunteering, somewhat driven by guilt. I come from a family that looked down on such people as "do-gooders." Not sharing their outlook, I tried to make up for what I perceived as a wrong. Luckily, there have been many opportunities to do this.

However, I have a tendency to overdo. Once, years ago, I was waiting to hear the results of a test to determine whether I had breast cancer. At the time, I thought with some relief, that if I did have cancer I would at least be able to drop all my commitments. If ever there was an "aha" moment, that was it. I had become so overwhelmed by excessive volunteering that I looked at cancer as the only way out. How extreme and ridiculous. That very day I started practicing how to say "no" so that, hopefully, I would not become so bogged down again.

Now, in my late seventies, I am ready to reduce my volunteer efforts even more. I need private, unscheduled days. I continue to help out here and there with, for instance, monitoring for invasive water plants, timing the 90-mile paddle race, or ushering at the local theater, but I am no longer willing to take on the responsibility of being an organizer or board member. Thankfully, many others do not resist the call and new generations step up. Those fine folks continue to make villages, such as Saranac Lake, the unique and delightful places they are.

Our children, my pottery and my writing are the best I can contribute. The children can speak for themselves, my ceramics and books must speak for me. I am delighted to see our offspring engaging in art, teaching, research, writing, architectural design, love of the outdoors and (oh joy) pottery making. I am grateful to have so many years in my pocket and to have the privilege of watching family members follow their own paths through life. Those paths can be rock-strewn, steep and tricky to maneuver. I am confident they can handle them. I only hope they will enjoy the good fortune that has come our way.

Life Circling to Earlier Times

Sometimes life loops around and takes us by surprise. In my younger years, I was critical of my father for delving into so many diverse avocations instead of concentrating on just one to become an expert. I realize now that I am just like him in that regard. I too have let myself be pulled in many directions. The result? I have a little knowledge about a lot, a lot of knowledge about little.

Through the years, I have moved further and further from the views of my parents. But the things I enjoy *doing* still hark back to my youth. Now, as then, I love spending time in the woods studying the flora and fauna, delight in lake paddling, value solitude and evenings on the screened porch listening to a thrush trill his lullaby. I enjoy music, art, and the quiet of early dawn. I continue to read, write and examine everything. I remain contrary. Most of these attributes come from my father. The storyteller in me, the socializing, my love of dance and laughter come from my mother. I see now how very much our lifestyle may be determined by heritage. We try all kinds of things but often settle back into what is most familiar; for example, in my case, reading instead of watching movies. Life circling. This has taught me to pay attention to folks' backgrounds. It is key to better understanding how others become who they are. It leads to more tolerance.

Another amazing circle: we learned that Howard's (our son-in-law's) father had commanded an air force squad that had parachute-dropped food packages to the desperately hungry Dutch at the end of WWII. It was his squadron that made the drop on the heath next to Wim's home. Wim's father had managed to squirrel away film during the war (by exchanging his tobacco rations) and had made an 8-mm movie of those drops as he and Wim watched from the ground. It was later converted to a DVD and Howard's father got to see it before he died. Who would have ever dreamed that the son of that squad commander would one day marry the daughter of that little boy watching from the heath. Life overflows with wonder.

The past steers the future. A case in point is that of a Kashmiri visitor to Saranac Lake who was unjustly detained in this country, spending part of his stay confined in a detention center. He could not receive phone calls, so many of us wrote to help keep up his spirits. I remembered how my own mother, years ago, had sent me weekly letters while I was detained in boarding school and what a difference that had made. So here was my chance to follow her example and pay that kindness forward. How we are raised determines much.

More circles. Sometime during his building years, Christopher had become good friends with Gordon Keyes, who built custom cabinetry for installation in Tissot Construction projects. They had known each other for about eight years when one day Christopher happened to mention our first names. Gordon's eyes opened wide on hearing "Caper and Wim." He had never made the connection. It turns out that we had rescued Gordon many years earlier in Bennington, VT when he had driven into town in his VW bus, promptly breaking down in front of our house. We invited him inside for tea and to find help for his vehicle. We became fast friends for several years until he moved away and we lost track of him. That was back during the '60s when nobody bothered with last names. Christopher was 7 years old at the time. Gordon had often babysat and given him guitar lessons. Now, many years later, neither of them had had a clue who the other was until our names came up. Gordon then went upstairs and produced, to Christopher's amazement, a postcard I had sent and a piece of pottery I had made years earlier.

I grew up spinning 78 rpm vinyl records before graduating to 33s and 45s. These were pushed out by cassette tapes, then CDs, access to music on computers and now MP3 players and phones that do everything but make your morning coffee. I admit it's all getting beyond me. I have returned to listening to the fine sound of 33 vinyls. New does not always mean better.

Now Jennifer and Christopher will soon retire. Christopher sold his business with its name, Tissot Construction, and its crew intact. Martha, no longer a professor, is becoming a writer. We only just retired ourselves a few years ago and now, blissfully early in their lives, our children are doing the same. Things circle around. How quickly the years roll by. Martha's husband Howard, unlike the rest of us, will most likely not stop until he can no longer heave himself out of bed to give another lecture. The rest of us are discovering the joys of leisure.

The past, both for me personally and on a larger scale, rolls back up time and time again. We could understand much if we paid attention to that fact.

And So ...

While the *activities* I enjoy are mostly a carry-over from my youth, *what* I believe and *how* I try to live have been determined by deliberately chosen values. Stealing quiet reflective moments away from frantic days has allowed me the time to reflect and make carefully considered choices. Had I insisted on being busy every minute, I would not have had the space to examine the how and why of my place in the scheme of things. A contemplative life has its rewards. We could all use more moments of silence.

The media increasingly intrude into our culture and with demanding voice, proclaim how we should live and what issues dominate. The lure of using the latest device has bullied its way into interrupting every conversation, gathering and peaceful moment. *Resist and rebel,* I say.

Today, hostile factions are fanning the flames of fear – leading to intolerance, dishonesty and violence against one another, as well as against the planet. Fortunately, new generations are stepping up to kick the cultural ball in a different direction. This gives me hope.

There are those who have kicked with good results, others, like myself, have mostly just kicked leaves. This is not a reason to stop trying. *How* we live matters. Until now, I have been lucky to come through the years relatively unscathed. Thanks to good health, a supportive family, adequate income and a partner with whom I share important activities and conversations – retirement has been rewarding. However, lucky or not, the hands on the clock go round and round, faster and faster. Nor can we stop them. Time gets us in the end. Our best defense? Kick, cry, rage, dance, laugh as long as we can and – like Motel 6 – keep the lights on for those who follow.